Born in 1967, Daniel Duane has climbed both the Northwest Face of Half Dome and the Nose route on El Capitan, and has worked as a climbing guide and instructor. He currently lives in Santa Cruz, California.

Lighting Out

A Vision of California and the Mountains

Lighting
Out

A Vision of California
and the Mountains

by

D a n i e l   D u a n e

The Grub Bag by Ida Jones was published by Random House.
Copyright © 1971 by Ida Jones.

Publication of this volume is made possible in part by a grant provided
by the Minnesota State Arts Board through an appropriation by the
Minnesota State Legislature, and by a grant from the National Endow-
ment for the Arts. Additional support has been provided by the Andrew
W. Mellon Foundation, the Lila Wallace–Reader's Digest Fund, the
McKnight Foundation, the Dayton-Hudson Foundation for Dayton's
and Target stores, the Cowles Media Foundation, the General Mills
Foundation, and other generous contributions from foundations, cor-
porations, and individuals. Graywolf Press is a member agency of
United Arts, Saint Paul. To these organizations and individuals who
make our work possible, we offer heartfelt thanks.

Published by Graywolf Press
2402 University Avenue, Suite 203
Saint Paul, Minnesota 55114
All rights reserved.
Printed in the United States of America.

A Graywolf Paperback Original

2 3 4 5 6 7 8 9
First Printing, 1994

Library of Congress Cataloging-in-Publication Data

Duane, Daniel King, 1967-
   Lighting out: a vision of California and the mountains
by Daniel King Duane
     p. cm.
   ISBN 1-55597-210-1
   1. Duane, Daniel King, 1967- . 2. Mountaineers—United States—
Biography. 3. Graduate students—United States—Biography.
4. Mountaineering—California. I. Title.
GV199.92.D93A3   1994
796.5'22'092—dc20
[B]   93-34067

for my parents,
Dick and Kit Duane
and for
Thomas Farber

"But I reckon I got to light out for the Territory ahead of the rest, because aunt Sally she's going to adopt me and sivilize me and I can't stand it. I been there before."

Mark Twain, *The Adventures of Huckleberry Finn*

One

On my last day before flying back out west, I had a final beer with the campus literary journal. A cold spring rain washed the windows of the old Albatross Pub as we toasted our fiction editor's acceptance to grad school at Yale. Post-Marxism, postmodernism—Drew was on his way. At an oak table under an autographed oar he told us about the honors thesis that got him in—political repression and human anatomy in two early British novels. Obscene and fascinating, it had been an unplowed field. Greek letters carved in the tabletop lay preserved beneath a coat of polyurethane; old photographs on the walls of pale rowing crews and muddy football teams were strictly black and white. Both California graduate schools I'd applied to had just axed me; two paper-thin envelopes had arrived together.

"Why only West Coast schools?" asked a diminutive and anxious grad student from India. He'd just dropped out and supported himself by handing out the *Worker's Vanguard* and ghost-writing essays—eighty bucks for an A, sixty for a B. I filled my cheeks with Ivy Stout and thought over how to answer without exposing my less-than-total commitment to the life of the mind, my flakiness. I just wanted to get away from angst-ridden winters and state parks the size of football fields. After I'd quit the fraternity, college had certainly improved—our journal had made a splash when Drew used margin text to create resonances between eco-feminism and fascism—but now I wanted to go home.

"I mean," Drew demanded, "you did only apply to West Coast schools, right?"

Grad school back East? My twenties in Providence? New Haven? Princeton? Baltimore? These were dying cities, but how to say to people who forgave my fraternity sins that I needed to live near mountains more than a few thousand feet high? And without farms and turkey hunters in them? So I swallowed my beer and said offhandedly that I just liked it better out there. Things were just, I don't know, more beautiful. Wide open spaces, and all that. The whole western world out of sight behind you if you wanted it there. And what a dump upstate New York seemed that afternoon—drizzling and cold in May; muddy, owned, farmed, crowded, fenced-off. Even after four years I couldn't get rolling hills and Appalachian villages to feel like home. And that morning my type-A girlfriend, a carnivorously intellectual sorority girl, had dumped me in the name of practicality—different coasts, different dreams. I had an airline ticket for the next morning, skipping graduation.

"I've been to California," Drew said. His head so outscaled the rest of his body that the whole black-turtle-necked arrangement tottered forward under the weight of his ivory jaw. "Yeah, my freshman-year roomate's place in Marin County. One of these BMW Deadheads with serious wealth in the woods and constant fresh-squeezed OJ. No poor people anywhere."

The gaunt poetry editor smirked and fingered his ponytail. Visions of Vineland, of hot-tubbing Aquarians—indelible and unassailable; I'd put some of these ideas in their heads with my talk of hot springs in the high mountains and pot plantations in redwood country. Places I wanted to get back to, or hadn't had enough of in the first place. A nativity I'd never fully aquired. The art editor, son of New York rural hippies, enormously muscular and wearing old army pants and a Tibetan vest, looked hopefully at me for a rebuttal. My vision of California had appealed to him, maybe a place to go after school. I looked out the window to where his battered blue-plaid VW bus was parked in the rain.

"Guy insisted on hiking clear to the top of Mount Tamalpais every night," Drew continued. "Pretty smashing sunsets looking way out to sea, and it's supposed to be some great power spot." Drew waved around a cigarette as he spoke, dropping ashes on the table and staining his slender fingers yellow. "He swore some beatnik poets went out there in the late fifties and marched around blowing on conch shells and chanting sutras or mantras or something, so locals think the place is sacred." I coughed a little from the smoke as my own version of Mount Tam came to mind—from Berkeley, it was a black-etched peak north of the Golden Gate lit by a burning aura from a late summer sunset. "After a week out there," Drew said, "I was chang-ing into somebody I didn't want to be."

The debate was my fault to begin with—playing the stage Californian when I'd failed at being Ivy League. The poetry editor looked evenly at Drew and me, weighing. A charismatic and emaciated neo-Marxist with a penchant for the occult, he'd grown up in Toronto and spent his sum-mers acting in London. He loathed Ithaca's provincialism and preferred the darkness of European cities—"shit" was happening there, changing, cops with submachine guns hung out at street corners. Sure, he'd been to a few sweat lodges with the local Black Turtle Indian Nation, but four years of hearing from me about the nature/culture split and the pristine beaches of Point Reyes had eroded his sympa-thy. I think my girlfriend had felt the same.

So I said I knew people in California who went to work every day and came home and paid bills and made love and got pissed at each other and it all seemed pretty real last time I was home. "It's just that when you're in a lovely place," I insisted, knowing it sounded ridiculous to the whole editorial board, "it changes how you think. Maybe just a little bit, but it does. Like photo-deprivation depres-sion. Or old doctors sending you to the south of France for cures."

The sutras on Mount Tam even sounded all right to me—we're a young culture, got to start sacralizing some-where. My own honors thesis had been on the poetry of na-ture and place, some of it deliciously misanthropic. I'd been looking west, had ignored all the relevant scholarship and followed the advice of an old professor: "Just say no to theory." They gave me lowest honors. Drew's critique of the dispersed exercise of power had gotten him a summa.

"And anyway," I said, "there's stuff I want to do out there before I get on the career track, like learn to climb."

"Climb?" Drew asked.

"Yeah. Rock climb. My dad's into it."

Drew took a long drink from his ceramic stein, then wiped his lips and smiled.

"The old WASP nostalgia for culture-free wilderness," he said, winking at the poetry editor.

T w o

Thinking how to light out and where to light out for, I wandered the crowds of Berkeley's Telegraph Avenue trying to see lives, jobs, spiritually survivable careers. Twenty-one years of "occupation: student" over. I stood in front of Blondie's Pizza, the smell of pepperoni overpowering sandalwood incense and car exhaust, and listened to a bearded man in a pink lace dress shout down a sidewalk evangelist. An irritated young man in a navy blue suit walked quickly past—he clearly had a job. Indoors. Summer, and he looked pale as he carried a banana and a sandwich off to spend his thirty free minutes on the student union steps. Without the big story of school—the firm calendar and regular punctuations of grades—did one just . . . just live? I'd heard of ex-cons who couldn't function outside the pen, of Navy Seals who rejoined weeks after discharge. I watched the young man pass, watched the calm behind his rimless glasses and looked for evidence of despair. He disappeared into the crowd and I fell down onto a bench with vertigo.

On my way to the airport in Ithaca I'd seen one of my old pledge brothers walking across the quad. As house president he'd acquired a swagger, but that morning it was different:

"Herb," I'd asked, "why do you look saddle sore? You know, walking bowlegged?"

"Oh, hey Opie," he'd said, "yeah, I got that job as a trader for Salomon Brothers and, ah . . . "—he spread both hands deep beneath his crotch like he was holding watermelons—"my 'nads are so big I can barely walk."

Mom said I ought to relax for a year, live at home and let the next step emerge. But that morning I'd found myself sitting in the same old house I grew up in while humanity was off at work. When I caught myself reading in the paper about a local water ordinance and a double suicide, my whole neck and chest constricted. I'd hustled out to sit in a café, but just got more and more wired without finishing my book. Even the summer riots had been a letdown: a homeless march martyring the guy killed in the '69 Free Speech Riots had turned into a looting frenzy by students, gangsters, homeless people and teenage skinheads who thought it was their Vietnam. News of an impending apocalypse, but bringing no particular story to an end.

Drinking a double espresso at a green slate and black iron table, I had waking nightmares of disappearing into a hermetically sealed office building all day, coming home at night; it was easy to give fraternity guys at school a hard time for selling out, for getting jobs on Wall Street making eighty grand a year at a hundred hours a week when work for me still meant reading *Ulysses*. But now? What to do? Everything lucrative went on behind airtight windows.

Guys twenty-one years old wore the same suits as the broken-down old-timers, both letting careers eat the whole
middle out of their lives. I'd passed a gym window that
morning full of people on stationary bicycles and wondered
what was so awful about motion, how they could stand to
resist it.

The star of our high school plays and designated hallucination tripmaster was already in Israel on a kibbutz. No
plans to return to Babylon. Two of my best friends had left
for Prague, the Paris of the nineties; another tired old city,
but at least they'd taken off. One was shooting black-and-
white photos of change, the other said he just wanted to
ruminate on his pain, maybe open a used bookstore. Nick
Cohen, my only friend equally interested in wasting time in
the mountains, wouldn't be back from college for another
week. Aaron Lehrman, the one hard-core mountaineer I
knew, wasn't around either. Aaron's dad, an embittered
local flamenco guitar teacher, said Aaron had dropped out
of artsy Reed College and hadn't called in a few weeks.
Aaron's mom, poetry editor of a Berkeley neighborhood
newspaper, thought he was somewhere out in the Rockies.
I had to get out of town fast, try to get roofing work in Lake
Tahoe for the summer. Winter in Jackson Hole, work at a
ski resort. Maybe save up and go to Nepal, wander through
the mountain kingdom like my dad's youngest brother,
Sean, had done at my age. There was a picture of him on
our living room wall, an unpleasant fierceness in his eyes as
he stood bearded in a blue down jacket beneath Shivling,
the sacred penis of the mountain god.

I drank the last of my cold, bitter coffee and tried to imagine the fabric of an office-bound day, the actual hours spent behind a desk reading in tedium, deferring gratification. Granted, an old complaint about the rat race, but so quickly it could add up to a life lived. Stopping at my table for just a moment with a decaf latté to go, a childhood friend insisted he was at peace with going to law school. Already dressing middle-aged, apparently leapfrogging his twenties with pleasure, he looked forward to getting the ball rolling. But civil torts, federal tax codes and contracts at twenty-one? Well, he was going to Europe for the summer by himself and thought he'd sow some oats over there, just in time to get down to business. It shouldn't have terrified me like it did—after all, it was his life—but I knew I had to get out of town.

Three

Hoping to find my dad and Uncle Sean up rock climbing in Yosemite, I packed my little blue pickup and drove out through the orchards and vineyards of the Central Valley toward Groveland. At Yosemite Junction in the foothills, the big range rippling up out of California's Kansas, I went south in the summer heat to where the Tuolumne River—a big, splashing stream running over white granite boulders and slabs—cut under a bridge.

I hit the brakes at a dusty turnout, hopped out, and grabbed a towel and a guitar. My sandals picking up pebbles the whole way down, I walked through poison oak and blackberry bushes to a swimming hole. An off-duty road crew had strung a steel cable from high rocks on one side of the deep pool to oak trees on the eroding hill opposite; a thick, frayed rope hung from the cable's midpoint down to the water. Coming up here with my mom, dad and sister when I was a kid, I'd thought of that cable as being about fifty, maybe even sixty feet off the water. Dad had to be crazy to climb out on it, swinging around like the teenagers. Mom would dive from some pretty high rocks, but she stayed away from the cable. He'd hang out there in space with his Levis on, kicking his feet around and whooping, then let go and slap into icy snow-melt water. As I got closer to the pool, I started dropping my height estimate on the cable, remembering that my preschool playground had recently turned out to be only about half an acre—not the two or three square miles I recalled. Sure enough—twelve feet, tops.

I lay out on the granite slabs getting sunburned, pinker and pinker all the time—the redhead's fantasy that maybe, just maybe, this'll be the year I get tan. Some local folks shotgunned malt liquors and started talking loudly about Bay Area white-bread yuppies running around the day before, thinking they were ballsy jumping off rocks. I took off my little round glasses.

A pockmarked old biker in a black leather vest and blunt-toed motorcycle boots threw a full can of beer into the blackberry bramble. Two men with turtle tattoos and long black hair took off their sneakers and T-shirts, but not their Levis. The older—probably in his forties—had two deep circular scars on his belly and a braided ponytail. The other, no more than twenty-five, had predatory blue eyes and a dark olive tan. They ran across the hot slabs to the shallow end of the pool while two women in matching terry-cloth tube tops—one pink and one blue—popped open Budweisers and leaned forward to watch. The men picked around in the shallows, turning over rocks for a while until they found what they wanted. Each picked up a chunk of granite about the size of a human head and then they started walking into the deep water side by side.

Everyone on the rocks leaned over to watch through the clear water. Walking upriver into the pool, the two men picked their way carefully across the bottom. Soon their chests were submerged, then their necks. They looked at each other a last time and took a deep breath before going under. As they sank below the surface their figures warped with the ripples above. A highway patrolman slowed as he crossed the bridge. The old biker took up a collection for beers and walked off toward the road.

"Crazy Indians, huh?" said the woman in blue. She lay back on her towel in the sun.

"Are these guys real Indians?" asked the other. "Indians hate water."

One of the men appeared to have fallen a step behind the other, and a few bubbles burst above him. A cloud shadowed the pool, and for a moment the men were hard to discern from the reflected hillside. Then the sun hit the water again and a cloud of bubbles exploded to the surface; one had stopped walking altogether. The woman in pink flashed a confused look at me, then back at the water.

With a splash the younger man burst up coughing and spitting. As he swam to the rocks, the older man walked out the other end of the pool. Only when he was standing dry on a boulder did he drop his rock. I gave up on the tan and sat under a bay tree, trying to remember bluegrass songs I'd played with my dad—"Black Mountain Rag," "Cripple Creek," "Old Joe Clark." He'd played banjo in a backyard country band for years and taught me to swap melodies with him on guitar. At the opening chorus of "Billy the Kid," the one about how at the age of twelve years Billy killed his first man, the old pockmarked biker looked straight at me and said "Hell. That's *my* music. You keep playing that shit."

When the crowd thinned out I drove off to a deli and picked up a rib-eye steak and a six-pack of rightly named Plank Road beer. The petrified mesquite in my little hibachi took forever to get hot, so I had nothing to do in that slow foothills sunset except throw gravel at bats and think about climbing. Not just peak-bagging this time either, but actually roping up. A handful of pebbles into a lodgepole pine sent clouds of fluttering shadows into the sky. A few bats dodged close like giant squeaking houseflies.

Four

Just before dawn I bolted upright in my sleeping bag, sweating from the heat that rose out of the Central Valley. I thought I'd heard something nearby, maybe a coyote, so I sat for a while, smelling the dust and pine and the faint residual exhaust coming off the road. A Sysco restaurant supply truck blew past toward Yosemite and I decided to get up. I thought again about my girlfriend and how I'd begged her to come out here with me after school, maybe drift around in the truck together for awhile. Go down to Mexico and space out on some beach. No interest.

In Groveland I stopped at a coffee shop with a blue-tiled floor for a waffle with ice cream and a side of bacon. At a big, round table, a man in new blue jeans and a clean white T-shirt, with a huge, hard belly and powerful hands, poured nonfat milk over a bowl of raisin bran. He listened to an unshaven older man in a green denim sportcoat and snakeskin boots talk about a Fourth of July fair, about how his son had paid five bucks for five sledgehammer swings at the Lincoln Continental but hadn't busted anything.

Then, farther east into higher mountains; colder, pine-scented air from still-blooming alpine meadows and evergreens replaced the arid dustiness of gallery oak forest and manzanita. An hour later, past the deep gorge of Yosemite Valley proper, the range stretched out in wide-open views to the north and south, hundreds of square miles of rocky peaks and forested valleys.

I remembered climbing the ancient winding stair to the top of Notre Dame during my junior year abroad: nothing but metropolis in all directions. At one smoggy horizon I saw another cathedral, Sacré-Coeur. The next day I took the metro out there. Again, sprawl to the horizon and I knew I couldn't do it, I couldn't stay. I read a used copy of *Walden* in Shakespeare and Company Books for a few days until I could get my tuition back in traveller's checks. I blew the chance of a lifetime and headed for the Pyrenees. Everyone loves Paris . . . and the chance to live there?

Alpine meadows at nine thousand feet: acres of green rock-garden, a meandering river, white granite domes bubbling out of the trees and broken white peaks reaching to over twelve thousand feet. Air noticeably thinner and colder, smelling still more of pine and summer. At 8:30 a.m. I pulled off Route 120 into the parking lot of the Tuolumne Meadows Grill, a white canvas building alone on the mountain highway. Four skinny guys in worn-out Patagonia jackets stood around playing Hackey Sack; their white cotton pants were shredded in places, reinforced in others. I wondered if they lived here year-round—they seemed adapted, as if they'd never thought of going anywhere else and had wasted no time getting here. A man and a woman in matching blue Lycra tights stretched their hamstrings in a patch of grass. A bleach-blond teenage boy sat in an open 1965 VW bus and ate granola from a plastic bag. Dad and Uncle Sean were drinking coffee in the sunshine at a picnic table and I could see Dad laughing as I killed the engine.

"The elevator-shaft drop," I heard Sean saying, as I walked toward them, "puts me right in the pit on this wave my buddy's too spooked to touch, so I'm ripping down the line at forty-five, pissing my trunks"—with one forearm he made the shape of a wave with the hand curling above while the other hand motioned along the side of it—"fully spooked the monster lip's going to close out and punish me, so I freak and bail off my board. Well . . . " he looked up at me and motioned with a finger to let him finish the story. "Well, on a fifteen-foot wave you can't just bail. That puppy shot me into the air like a rag doll and while I'm falling I'm thinking, 'OK. This is the part where I die. The coral reef's definitely going to Cuisinart me this time.'"

Dad pulled me down next to him at the picnic table and put his heavy arm around my shoulders. His hands were covered with athletic tape and scabs and his hazel eyes were alive and calm like they never were in town. He and his brother were both darker-skinned than I was and both had dark brown hair, but Dad was balding and he was shorter and thicker than Sean. Sean was my height— almost 6'3"—and had more angular features and a broad, thin-lipped smile over perfect teeth. He took a sip of coffee, then went on. "So twenty thousand gallons slam me toward the reef but for some amazing reason my back slams down against the only patch of sand in the bay. I was like, 'sheeeeeit, this place ain't shit.' Hey, Danny! You look a little pale, you got the flu, or what?"

They were up training in the Meadows to climb the Northwest Face of Half Dome—the ultimate aspiration of their shared alternate life. Three full days on a wall, sleeping on ledges, climbing from dawn to dusk. They'd been working up to it the whole time I'd been in college and were finally ready. They'd gone through a long series of practice climbs, a program of steps and trials. Dad got some more eggs on a paper plate and they talked about how ready and how scared they both actually were. It was an enormous, world-famous wall, maybe just enormous enough to ease the frustrations of their urban lives.

Sean had come up for the climb from San Diego, where he and his wife lived by the beach. At forty he was surfing three times a week, running ten miles a day and, at his wife's insistence, seeing a therapist about his Peter Pan complex. He'd been enjoying selling wine for two California wineries—driving up and down the state, skiing in Tahoe when he made winter sales trips to the resorts, climbing in the Meadows when he had to come up to Mammoth in the summer. Sean had also patiently taught me how to surf when I was a kid. We'd camped out in his little car in a parking lot by a nuclear power plant at San Onofre and he spent a whole day showing me how to spring to my feet. It took a while to stick, though, because up north where I lived it was more about character-building than fun-in-the-sun: fogbound rocky coastline with pounding Pacific waves, frigid water. He said it'd be a soul-surfing experience up there if I could ever get good enough for the bigger winter swells. Fewer kooks in the water, fewer Nazis.

Five

At sparkling Tenaya Lake, Dad, Sean and I walked up shining slabs to Stately Pleasure Dome. Dad walked evenly, with his head down, placing his feet carefully as the rock steepened. He wore blue canvas shorts and a red T-shirt and had an old blue rope coiled around his shoulder. My little day pack was crammed with all this great stuff that Dad stored on hooks out in the garage: rock-climbing shoes, a sit-harness, a bag of gymnastic chalk to keep the hands dry of sweat, thirty or forty snap-link carabiners, little metal wedges on cable loops for sticking in cracks in the rock—called chocks, nuts or stoppers, contraptions called "Friends" with four quarter-circle cams—when you pulled a trigger the cams pulled back, when you released it they expanded into a crack.

Dad strapped me into this elaborate nylon harness and made me watch him do the buckle—apparently if you blew it, the thing could dump you. Sean went straight to work, muttering to himself while he organized the rest of the gear. It seemed like he had some routine he was running through, some whole program he and Dad had worked out.

"While I climb," Dad said, pulling a little white cap

over his bald spot, " . . . you listening? While I climb, Sean feeds me rope, OK? And if I peel off, Sean's got this brake so it stops feeding. That's my whole life right there in that guy's hand."

"Come on, man . . . get going," Sean said. He looked over at me in annoyance, sick of the first child's thoroughness.

Dad tied into the rope and led off up the wall. At more than twice my age, he was in way better shape. While he climbed, the rope trailing from his harness down to Sean, I watched him put chocks in little cracks in the rock. He'd clip a carabiner to the chock, then clip the rope below him through the carabiner. I got to wondering just how badly I actually wanted to do this. The stakes seemed pretty high. Back down at the lake a couple of kids were floating around in inner tubes.

"Guy's tenacious," Sean said. "Yesterday he kept blowing off this overhang, bleeding and yanking me all over the place. But he kept at it. I would've been out of there." I tried to imagine Dad dangling upside down by his fingers, tried to gauge the truth-content of the remark; it was certainly possible.

Dad did most of the work on this route with his feet, just kind of walking up the rock.

"All right," Sean said, "your turn, Danny. How do those rock shoes feel?"

"Horrible." They were mashing my curled up toes together and the seams were excavating trenches on the tops of my feet.

"How bad?"

"Really horrible. Like, I may never walk again."

Sean laughed, enjoying his hardman posture. "Then they're way too loose," he said. "No kidding. And take my chalk bag."

"You think I'll need it?"

"I don't know, you're so scared already your palms are dripping. You don't want to grease off, do you?"

Not at all. Nope. Not even a little bit. I clipped the bag onto my harness and shoved both hands in there. White courage.

As I climbed, just kind of walking upwards, focused like a madman, my knees shaking, Sean yelled, "Keep breathing! Don't stop breathing!" Astonishing that Dad got a kick out of this, not to mention it being irresponsible for a man with children. Dad grabbed my hand when I got close and hauled me in, then immediately attached my harness to the anchor he'd built. Sean climbed after us, pulling up with long swimmer's arms.

They fumbled with equipment and knots for a while, getting ready for the next "pitch"—the next rope-length of climbing. I remembered that Dad had learned the rope system from an eccentric old climber in Berkeley who was quasi-religious about safety. As the bright blue day wore on, and I watched these two brothers work together, I could tell safety had become a discipline of its own for Dad—knots always backed up, carabiner gates always down and away from the rock, double 'biners opposed and reversed, ropes well coiled and neat—a litany of details, of logical checks and balances.

At a little ledge up there in the cool mountain wind and thin-atmosphere sunshine, Dad talked me through every step in the chain of self-protection. He laid out rules with moral intensity: never clip like this, always like this; absolutely never commit to two pieces of protection, always three; never, ever unclip from an anchor when you're not on belay; never let anyone unclip you; always look over an anchor, no matter who's built it. The system made sense and I imagined if you stayed manic about it, climbing could be survivable. I pictured all the long days Dad had spent moving over stone far away from his job and life, engaged in a system rhythmic enough for his usually constricted, uneven breathing to follow suit, absorbed in the running of ropes, the tying of knots, the fitting of steel into stone.

Near the top I got confused as to where to move and had to dip my hands a few times in the chalk. I couldn't see anything to hold onto or any particular place to put my feet. My stomach knotted up, and I looked around for what hold Dad had used. The gray-and-white rock was speckled with mica and feldspar. Sections were polished by glaciers to the smoothness of glass; they reflected the sun like the mirrors sewn on one of my old girlfriend's fraternity date-night dresses.

"Trust the shoes," Sean said, like telling me to use the force. "They'll stick."

He was right—the rubber held better than sneakers on pavement, and after a few steps my eyes wandered away from the granite around me. That huge, wild white dome up in the sky dropped gently back down to the banks of blue

Lake Tenaya; above, it curved away into an equally blue horizon. To either side, more walls of this pure, clean, pale
stone lay against the air—the raw stuff of the High Sierra,
stark and clean, and I was wandering around on it with my
dad and uncle and with nowhere to be but right there. And
so terrified I couldn't help but focus; I hadn't thought about
much but a rock in over an hour.

When I reached Dad at the summit I laughed involun-
tarily. Berkeley? Light out? College?

"Fun, huh?" Dad said.

A pale man with white hair appeared climbing below
me in shorts and a T-shirt. No rope. The guy had to be
nuts—one slip and he'd die. Dad nodded at me, as if to say,
Damn straight that's crazy. The guy smiled in noblesse-
oblige friendliness, like he found us charming and wanted
us to know it was OK to use ropes. Then he moved past.
While I caught my breath, a man with a beer-belly in a powder-blue T-shirt and a wiry, muscular woman also appeared
without ropes. Soon they were gone out of sight, walking
down the backside of the dome.

We stood for a while in the breeze and reorganized the
gear. A thunderhead shadowed half the lake. Sean taught
me how to coil a rope so it wouldn't tangle and could be carried comfortably. I stood next to him and matched the
movements of his hands until I got it. The views were ludicrous: ranges of white and alpine green reaching from the
brown haze of the Central Valley and foothills off to the
cobalt atmosphere over the barren crags of the higher
mountains. Ten miles west, Dad and Sean's grail: the huge

rounded tower of Half Dome. Sean shivered with pleasant fear.

As we walked down broad orange-and-tan ramps and boulders, muscles loose and tired, I saw the three-some who'd climbed past without ropes. On a block looking out toward Half Dome they sucked on a bong and smiled into space.

S i x

Across the street from People's Park, in front of the People's
Cafe where the coffee was always free, someone with
muddy hands slashed the roof of a badly rusted, green con-
vertible Karman Ghia and ran off with a backpack and
sleeping bag. Kyla White, the woman who'd been robbed,
was moving back up to Berkeley for the summer from the
University of California at Santa Cruz. Looking for replace-
ments, she came into the small, expensive mountaineering
store where I'd just gotten a job. Formerly a Russian Ortho-
dox church and wedding chapel, the old building had shin-
gled turrets and stucco walls impregnated with flagstones.
Inside, mountaineering equipment and Gore-Tex rainwear
hung on racks on hardwood floors beneath vaulted ceilings.

When I first noticed Kyla, she was chewing a fingernail
where the wedding altar now held sleeping bags. She happened to be right under this absurd inscription in a cross-
beam that read, "Love Never Faileth," and I edged out
another employee, our backcountry ski guru, to ask her if
she needed help.

"No thanks," she said, without looking at me.

"Any questions about anything?"

"No, really, thanks."

I walked back to the register to regroup and took a sip of water. She had piles of curly blond hair, some of it corn-rowed, some of it dreadlocked, and her eyes were open and green, though slightly depressed. She wore a black leotard under a torn white T-shirt, ripped jeans and running shoes, and looked like she was in great shape. Probably jogged on some beach at sunrise daily to fight off whatever was putting those shadows under her eyes.

"Dan," the fascist manager said, irked and out of touch as usual, "why don't you go make sure that woman doesn't have any questions?" She'd moved into the backpack room and was reading a hang-tag on a red-and-black Mountain-smith.

"Look," I said to her, just doing my stupid job, "can't I tell you something about packs?" This time she yielded, and I gave her this whole rap I'd learned about how most inter-nal frame packs put the weight on the small of your back but, see, ours load it onto your hips, right there . . . and right there. She also wanted a warm new sleeping bag, but didn't like any of our colors. She told me about the theft and I asked why she'd been in Santa Cruz.

"Crazy story," she told me. She leaned over to look in-side a Dana Designs Hyalite pack.

"I'd love to hear it," I said, "I mean, shit. Lay it on me."

She looked at me a little curiously, at my khakis and electric-blue tie-dye, then told me how she'd transferred down to the University at Santa Cruz after starting at UC

Berkeley. "At Berkeley I lived in this hippy co-op," she explained, "called Barrington where I really freaked out." She shook her head a little at the memory, like she'd either had a nervous breakdown or had gone on some mad collegiate sex-and-drugs binge. She sat on a cabinet and played with the hair on her legs while I asked what the problem was.

"Both the whole big city scene," she said, "and how Barrington was more of a shooting gallery than a commune. There was always some random, freaky dude wandering the halls doing speed. At first I got off on it, like I knew I wanted strangeness but not what kind? People'd like disappear into the heroin dens upstairs and you wouldn't see them until they showed up in the kitchen three days later eating cold hot dogs. And I'm like trying to organize communal vegan meals. What a joke."

She tried on every pack we had while I sat on the gray carpet and watched. She'd get one on her hips and feel it out, sort of walk around and bounce on each foot. She looked like she'd put up with a heavy load, but wanted it comfortable. While she took a spin around the shop with an ArcFlex Astral Plane pack, I got to thinking about how I was in sales. Just like my buddies in investment banking, except at the bottom. Working with great gear, but nonetheless, in sales, folding T-shirts and trying to laugh when a witty customer asked if we had Gore-Tex toilet paper. I asked what she had in mind after college.

"I don't know, just screw around. Definitely not get some fancy soul-death job in the city. My fantasy right now's to live on an organic farm." I'd never much thought about farming myself, but I decided on the spot I could be open to it. It turned out her folks were pushing for graphic arts or advertising, one of those feminine white-collar fields. "That's why Barrington freaked me out so much," she said, "here I'm coming from totally homogeneous Walnut Creek, with these dysfunctional conservative parents, my dad on the perpetual business trip, and like three black people in my whole high school. All of a sudden there's homeless people sleeping in my hallway! I wanted to be able to deal with that, and I'd been dying to get out of suburbia, which I totally hate." She stretched her arms up over her head and rolled her hips around in a circle, then said, "I realized, though, that I'm more looking for pretty places." Suddenly she looked me up and down. "Why?" she asked, "Where are you from?"

I told her I was from here but that I'd been gone for awhile in upstate New York. She'd heard of a self-supporting women's organic farm north of Ithaca and wanted to know if I'd been there. I hadn't, but the poetry editor had told me about it; they had a uniquely stable blend of goddess worship and communalism. Kyla'd also done a lot of backpacking in the Sierra. Climbing sounded neat to her, and she was amazed I'd done it with my dad. She'd love to try it. I asked her again how she got from Berkeley down to Santa Cruz.

"I felt so bad about all the privileged things I grew up with," she said, putting weighted sandbags into a pack, "that I felt guilty about every homeless person I saw, until my skin was like totally breaking out and I was getting this big black hole inside. There's also a stronger women's community down in Santa Cruz. I'm just up here for the summer—moving back down in a month."

"Women's community?" I started to snicker as I asked, then realized she was serious. She caught something of the tone and looked at me warily before answering.

"Yeah. Just a strong lesbian scene," she said, nodding affirmatively and searching my eyes. I tried to change my reaction fast—I was dying to ask her to coffee. "I'm not necessarily a lesbian," she said, "but that kind of atmosphere's really empowering."

I stuffed and unstuffed a few ArcFlex Terraplane packs, told her about the compression and stabilization strap, about the delta straps and the load nodes. I pulled out the pack's aluminum stay and custom bent it to the curvature of her slender back. I had to place the stay against her spine and run my finger down her T-shirt next to it until I was sure the fit was flush. It took a few tries to get it right.

"How do you like living in a small beach town?" I asked from behind her, meaning Santa Cruz. She had a purple-and-blue yin-yang patch on the back pocket of her ripped jeans.

"I have a beautiful life down there," she said, "sounds like you'd love it. You should come down. Although, actually, none of my friends in Berkeley really accept it, like it's not real to them."

"I have no realness hang-ups," I told her. "None."

"Well, they just think it's all happy, mellow white people signing petitions. Seems pretty real to me, and I don't see why living in a pretty place can't be real. It's kind of a direction I want to go, anyway." She looked at my sandals for a moment. I mentioned the skepticism of the editorial board toward the whole notion of California. She'd never lived anywhere else, but liked California pretty well.

"Also, destructive relationships with men," she said, "had a lot to do with my moving down there."

We sat together on the carpet in the pack room, mannequins swinging ice axes into the Romanesque vaults overhead, and she talked about a house of skylights in a Santa Cruz redwood grove, how she mountain biked to campus every morning on dirt trails with breezes blowing off the Pacific. Her first class was yoga in an octagonal redwood-and-glass room out in a meadow—so powerful she had to walk her bike afterwards for fear of crashing.

In the end, Kyla decided to just rent a backpack and think about buying one later; after all, it was a big investment. She hesitated for a moment, blinking at the sunlight beyond the door, the empty old rental pack on her back, then waved good-bye with her slender fingers and walked out. I stood for a moment and watched her walk down the steps and into the old Ghia. Just as she pulled out, with the top down on that funky, curvy old car, she caught me looking at her. She smiled just slightly to herself, and drove off. I ran back through the shop, past the Gore-Tex jackets and telemark ski boots, past the rock-climbing shoes and ice axes and straight into the rental area. I pulled her triplicate rental form back out of the accordion file, glanced around, and copied down her work number.

Seven

The next morning was foggy and cold, and I drove my pickup clear across congested Berkeley to just happen by the French bakery where Kyla worked. Among antique cases of exquisite morning buns and walnut-raspberry scones, kiwi tarts and strawberry tartlettes, she waited on a line of unhurried pensioners and frantic commuters. With beads braided into her cloud of uncombed blond hair and six earrings in her left ear, she described with perfect ease how they rolled out the croissant dough again and again to layer in the butter. She glanced up as I walked in, but went on selling a cappuccino and brioche to an old woman in a cashmere coat.

"I was wondering," I said, when she had a moment free, "if you'd get a drink with . . . ," she was shaking her head. "What?" I asked.

"I really don't like bars," she said. She leaned forward on the counter and looked at me carefully.

"A cup of coffee?" I asked. "No?" She shook her head again. "You don't drink coffee? Well . . . you could get tea! Even herbal tea, I'm sure . . . "

"How about just a walk?" she asked. She smiled with the corners of her mouth, though not with her eyes.

"A walk? You mean . . . go walking?"

"Yeah. A walk. In the woods, tonight."

"I . . . I'd love to. I love walking."

She picked me up at my parents' house and we drove up into the Berkeley hills. We strolled out a fire road with a view of San Francisco's lights reflected in the black pool of the bay. I remembered Mom telling me about coming up here to make out with Dad when they were in college. Kyla's black cowboy boots gave her a swinging stride, though they kept slipping on smooth spots. In a eucalyptus grove there were caches here and there of homeless people's possessions. Kyla said the trees were from Australia and had crowded out a lot of native species. A sallow man in a three-piece suit who was lying on the springs of a rotting couch paid little attention to us. Without pedantry, she pulled leaves off plants and offered them to taste—mugwort, yerba santa, sage—some bitter, some sweet. I'd hiked in those hills since I could walk and had never known the names of anything except poison oak and blackberries.

Lying in a meadow and bundled up inside her black turtleneck sweater, Kyla pointed out Orion and the Seven Sisters. She said she was an Aquarius, but didn't know where that was in the sky.

"Apparently," she said with mock-intimacy, "Aquarius means I'm independent and unattached, capricious and whimsical but not fiery. Can't, I assure you, be held down."

"Is that what you're like?"

"I don't know. Maybe."

Trying to sound neither convinced nor mocking, I offered that I was a Scorpio. She didn't respond. I waited a while, wondering as much how I'd meant the offer as about how she'd taken it. Maybe she was trying to remember the chemistry between Aquarians and Scorpios. Maybe it was supposed to be terrible. Or great. Or maybe she had no idea.

"Do you do a lot with astrology and crystals and stuff?" I asked. There was a pause while she thought about it. A siren sounded in the city below and I tried to make up my mind what I'd think if she said yes. My girlfriend in college, now working eighty-hour weeks in Manhattan, would've howled with laughter.

"Sometimes," she said. I waited a few minutes again. She didn't elaborate. Must just be second nature to her, I thought, and maybe that isn't so bad. Then she coughed lightly and said, "Yeah, funny stuff, huh? But there must something in it."

"Yeah, I've thought about it some too," I said, which wasn't really true. "This old hippy friend of my mom's said I was the only one in our family with an ancient soul. She said I'd been around a long time. Like pretty much since the beginning." That part was true. My folks had been a little put off because the sage hadn't had nearly as much to say about them.

"Hmm," she responded, without looking at me. She twirled a strand of hair between her fingers, her eyes still on the stars. I looked at her profile for a while, wondered whether she was serene or just shy. She didn't look back. I never had the guts to try kissing on first dates, and anyway, I had no idea what Kyla'd think if I did. I might have seemed like just another one of those over-aggressive guys she'd had enough of.

As she drove the Ghia through the forest, both of us freezing in the wind and the radio blaring Led Zeppelin, she rocked her head up and down and laughed at the music. She said she was going up to Yosemite for a few days, and maybe she could see me when she got back. I was going to Yosemite too, to climb, and I asked if we could meet in a meadow one day. I could show her how to climb, or maybe we could camp together or cook a meal. She'd love to, she said, but it was a women's music festival she was going to and a girlfriend had bought her the ticket.

Eight

Nicholas Cohen put a bare, hairy foot up on the dirty dashboard of my pickup and talked about the college back east where he'd just dropped out. I stayed in the passing lane south out of forested, foggy Berkeley and through sprawling, asphalt Oakland. No love lost, Nick said, but just like me he was psyched to be home. Then, six-lane Route 580 cut east out of the Bay Area and dry California grass appeared on hills denuded, reshaped, terraced; blasted out for the highway. In the valleys of the Coastal Range, housing tracts started and the air became dry and hot: California proper. Hundreds of square miles of just-add-lots-of-water neighborhoods.

"The clincher," Nick said, "was when this Betty-no-brainer sorority girl, or chick, or . . . woman, or whatever, that I met at a frat party. I only talked to her for a minute. She calls me up out of the blue and says, like she's going to make my year, 'Nick, I've talked to some guys I know, and I really, honestly think you're Sigma Chi material. I mean that.' I almost got hives." Nick rolled down the window and wiped dust off his gold wire-rimmed glasses. He wore a batiked polo shirt that made his gray eyes seem faintly purple. He actually was Sigma Chi material and was trying to fight it. Something about the attendant expectations of machismo were too much for him; he'd been trying to figure out how to tell his parents he wanted to paint, to make things with his hands. Handsome as hell, his only vanity was around his looks—otherwise he was petrified of criticism.

An isolated tract of faux-brick townhouses crowded against an oak forest; without a car and a tank of gas you wouldn't be able to get a cup of milk.

"Man, dude, you missed initiation," I said. "The big moment. Bonding with the boys and becoming a man. Republican, sports-fan nobodies in clean Levis, clean white sneakers and baseball caps."

"Your choice, my snotty friend," Nick said. He twisted my rearview mirror around to have a look at his freshly cut hair. "Right? You didn't have to do it. Don't pretend you had to do it. In fact, I bet you loved it."

"I asked one of my pledge bros why he rushed our frat," I went on, ignoring Nick's ridiculous insinuation, "and he said, 'Hey, you wouldn't call your country a cunt, now would you? So don't call your fraternity a frat.'"

A white gateway stood like a football goalpost over a road going nowhere: California prairie redefined as the Hacienda Business Park.

"Wait," Nick demanded, "aren't you the guy who dated exclusively DeeGees all four years of college?"

He had me. "Technically, that's true. But most of them

were Greek exiles like myself."

Nick exhaled heavily and nodded: "How Bohemian."

Santa Rita County Jail sprawled below curved folds and smooth rises of golden hillside. My mother once spent a weekend locked up there with six hundred other women for protesting nuclear weapons research at Lawrence Livermore Laboratories. She didn't like to talk about it much, but they'd kept the women together in a huge wooden gymnasium for three days. The guards brought in carts of paperback novels and four of the women got so pissed at the content, at the gender-casting and bullshit archetypes in that brainwashing crap they'd decided to burn the books in an act of protest, a localized tactic of resistance. Once the blaze was under way in a garbage can my mother risked social suicide by pointing out that all the doors of that sixty-year-old sun-baked tinderbox were chained and locked.

"Let me tell you about the joys you've passed up," I said, about to speak the unspeakable and break a solemn fraternity vow of silence. "The bros took all of us pledges out to a canvas tepee in the woods, dumped us with a keg, and said they'd come back in the morning and the keg better be empty. So we're supposed to get tight with each other for the hell that lies ahead."

Nick hadn't seen me in a while, and he took a long look at me. He remembered me mostly from High School water polo, for which he'd tried out, immediately made varsity, then quit because of the pressure to perform. His grandfather was a Freudian therapist in New York, his father an estranged Jungian in California. Nick had struggled as a

business administration major and had hung out in Boston
with the heirs of two New York department store families
doing blow and eating sushi nightly on their parents' Gold
Cards. Even that memory embarrassed him now, as if he'd
played a role in a bratpack film that flopped. He shifted his
feet on the dashboard and put his calfskin wallet in the
glove box.

The only road sign more frequent than "Speed Limit
55" was "Available." Housing tracts took names from whatever they'd bulldozed—Muir Field Estates, Meadow Glen
Single Family Homes, Blossom Valley Luxury Single Family Homes, Quail Ridge.

"So anyway, Red," Nick said, "what happened with the
keg?"

"A keg for fourteen guys turns out to be about ten
beers each," I explained. "A bonfire's raging in a pit outside
the tepee. I'm now hammered and kind of sick, and me and
this guy Marty from Michigan are doing bingers in the
woods—low-profile because the bros are uptight about pot.
Habitual sex offenders, stone alcoholics, but no pot smok-
ing and church on Sundays."

Two hundred blackbirds wobbled about a fallow field
in the old homestead wind shelter of six eucalyptus; the
farmhouse had long since vanished—"For Sale, Planned
Development. Inquiries from Principals Only." Ahead the
highway rose in a black line from the Livermore Valley to
the dry Coastal Range. On either side of the road ahead
something moved—the hills, then the entire crest of the
range shimmered in black. Twenty minutes later groves of

streamlined metal windmills with airline propellors for blades appeared on both sides of the highway. All of them spinning. Another five minutes and hundreds upon hundreds of fluttering towers infested the hills. Western rangeland, the last stretch of mountains before the great Pacific Ocean, reforested by tax accountants.

Now over the Coastal Range and down into the flat humidity of the Central Valley, we passed through Tracy and Manteca, towns with slaughterhouses and feed-lots the size of army bases. The rank, mulchy stench of blood flooded in and lingered long after we'd closed the windows. On the straight-line highway past thousands of acres of square, easy-packing tomatoes, the Word of Truth Fellowship had let things fall apart; its orange stucco had faded. On the other side of the beautifully wooded Stanislaus river, across the street from the grain elevator, Oakdale, California, on a sign: Optimists, Rotarians, Lions, Jaycees, the Oakdale Garden Club, Veterans of Foreign Wars, PofH Grange, International Order of Odd Fellows, Loyal Order of the Moose, Toastmasters International, Civitan, Kiwanis. After a bleak four-lane strip of franchises, Route 120 left the Central Valley and rose into the foothills—the gentle rise of the Sierra's western slope.

"So we're all standing around the fire," I said, "and guys are going around saying things about themselves. They're really nervous about it because they barely know each other, but somehow they can believe that this matters. They're talking about how 'my mom and dad broke up last year, and like, it's been really rough, but I'm all right. Yeah, I'm all right. I'm all right.' And all the guys are getting choked up and going, 'Dude, we're really here for you. That's great you can tell us.' But all this out there in the woods at a tepee, right?"

Nick looked deeply touched. He stuck a finger into his mouth to pull out a piece of tortilla chip, and said in garbled voice, "Robert Bly's got nothing on the Psi Gams of Cornell, does he?"

A red sun expanded into the dust of the valley behind us, melted and grew redder as we drove, blotted out the rearview mirror and highlighted Nick's straight, shiny black hair. They say you used to be able to see across California, from Mount Diablo in the Coastal Range to Mount Ritter on the eastern crest of the Sierra and up north to Shasta, a volcanic cone at the southern end of the Cascade Range. Hundreds of miles. The Sierra were named "nevada"—snowy—by a Spaniard who stood atop a peak by the sea and beheld a snow-capped range of mountains in the distance. This view occurs perhaps once every few years now, after a long storm, after much wind. So clear were the nineteenth-century skies, so beautiful the play of the sun across the peaks, John Muir called the Sierra the "Range of Light." Just as the new world was neither new nor China, just as the Indians were certainly not Hindus, snow does not, by any stretch, characterize that range of mountains whose banal Spanish descriptive has become an English proper noun.

"When it got to my buddy Marty, he pauses, so everyone gets real quiet, and all you could hear was the fire crackling and guys burping a little from the beer, and Marty's got this great midwestern poker face and he goes, 'Well, when I was only eight years old,' and with a totally straight face, 'I walked into the bathroom, and saw my father masturbating,' and he looked everyone in their blown-away eyes for a minute, then said, 'and ever since then I've been revolted by the sight of the human penis.' And he just stopped. Dead serious. Making the whole thing up."

"You sure?" Nick demanded.

"Of course! I mean, I think so, but anyway, these guys were appalled, but it was their game. None of them got the joke. They all came over and started putting their arms around him, saying, you know, 'We're really here for you, buddy,' and feeling the depth of their magnanimity for a bro. I was off behind a tree trying to pull my face out of a stoned perma-smile."

Nick looked out the window. He laughed a little for my sake, but I could tell something about the story made him uncomfortable. A new sign had appeared among foothills ranch country: Hatler Industrial Park. A hillock was gone and a bulldozer sat idle in the sun. A trailer home rusted among bicycle frames; two rotting green pickups sat on cinder blocks. As we drove past, a big man with a garden hose stood out among open, prone refrigerators and watered his dog.

"Sounds like a wild time," Nick said, riding his hand out the window like a plane. At once vulnerable and viciously critical, he was a great athlete who never liked team sports, a photographer who shot only strangers and never showed his work. Something about climbing struck just the right note for him—slightly renegade, no competition, individualistic. Grace was probably a plus.

The grass everywhere on those baking hot foothills was gnawed to the ground. At Chinese Camp, an old gold rush town, a family had moved into the church. Their laundry hung in the sun out back by the highway. A pagoda—wide-roofed and multicolored—stood apart in a field beyond town. Farther, the south fork of the Tuolumne River surged over boulders deep in its canyon.

Lake Don Pedro, a tremendous reservoir for the City of San Francisco, had lowered after years of drought. Once-submerged hillsides dried out in the sun. Drowned oaks—leafless, lifeless—stuck out above the water, leaned off the slopes in a grayness alien to the green and tan chapparal. Parking lot for houseboats, the lake's shrinking waters were crowded with those seeking solitude. Like squalid, aluminum-sided mobile homes, they floated in glaring sunlight. The boaters still swam, still lived the good life.

At the town of Big Oak Flat a stone cairn held three chunks of the original big oak. Not cross sections, just fireplace-sized chunks from when they'd cut it down for the new road. A band played bad rock-and-roll at California's oldest saloon—the Iron Door—and a woman with meaty shoulders and bloody hands danced drunk in the street with her old man. In one of those sight-bites you get as you drive fast through other people's stationary lives, a red-headed teenager vomited pink into a park barbeque.

Along a side road that led to flooded Hetch Hetchy canyon—the loss of which they say broke John Muir's spirit—we pulled over to sleep: just outside Yosemite National Park, ranger-free. In the morning, on in.

N i n e

epic: ep-ic \'ep-ik\ adjective [L epicus, fr. Gk epikos, fr. epos word, speech, poem] 1: of, relating to, or having the characteristics of an epic. 2a: extending beyond the usual or ordinary especially in size or scope. b: Heroic. Noun. 1: a long narrative poem in elevated style recounting the deeds of a legendary or historical hero (the Iliad and the Odyssey are epics) 2: a work of art (as a novel or drama) that resembles or suggests an epic 3: a series of events or body of legend or tradition thought to perform the proper subject of an epic (the winning of the west was a great American epic). And now, verb—"to epic."

Nick's feet fell hard off the dashboard. He sputtered "Oh, God . . . me," rolled down his window, and climbed out. First his head, then his arms, then his whole upper body was out of the vehicle with his Birkenstocks kicking around near the stick shift. I looked back at the road. Beyond a broad meadow, above a line of trees, something a mile away filled the windshield. A wall. A big, big, wall. I leaned forward to look up. It still filled the windshield; I got my neck over the steering wheel and still I couldn't lean far enough to see the top.

I hit the brakes and Nick grabbed the windowsill to keep from falling out altogether. We opened our doors simultaneously, turned off the radio and stood barefoot in the gravel. Three thousand feet high and a mile long. And vertical. Twice the height of the World Trade Center and much, much cleaner of line. Higher than safe cruising altitude for skydiving. More than half a vertical mile. Swirls of bright white-and-gold granite the size of towering thunderheads in the sun. We stood next to the truck and I felt my palms moisten. I wiped them off on my pants without looking away, but they kept sweating.

Nick walked forward a few steps in the gravel, took a step left, gestured helplessly with his hands, then looked back at me. "El Cap, huh?" he said.

"Mmm."

"Fuck that, eh?"

It did look pretty frightening, the thought of trying to get up on that monster. We drove on into Yosemite, slowly, both our heads out the windows of the truck. The valley rose wildly to glacial headwalls—the flatiron of Sentinel Rock, Yosemite Falls spraying into a thousand feet of air, and the crown jewel looming over the far end of the valley—Half Dome. A mountain of forest and stone lifted its rounded two thousand foot face far up over placid Mirror Lake, pushing the summit to nearly five thousand feet over the valley floor. Dad and Sean had taken a day longer than they'd planned and looked pretty bad when they got home. They both felt that El Cap—the ultimate rock climb—was beyond them. The whole scene felt beyond me.

We unloaded at the climbers' camp—officially called

Sunnyside Walk-In—unofficially Camp 4, after a cramped sleeping ledge high on El Capitan. Tents from all over the world crowded together on pine needles beneath sequoias. Picnic tables were strewn with beer bottles, jars of salsa, half-empty cans of beans and bags of cookies. In front of nearly every tent was a pile of great-looking equipment, of ropes, hammers, Friends. On the bulletin board at the ranger's kiosk were notes scrawled on torn scraps of paper: "climbing partner needed, I lead 5.10, follow 5.11," "Partner needed for Zodiac, must have PortaLedge and jugs," "Swiss girl needs ride to Modesto," "If I had a car I'd give you a ride," "I have a beard, and I'll give you a ride."

With Nick's little blue tent pitched, we sat out in the morning sun on the tailgate of the truck and sorted gear. Everywhere were climbers, bullshitting the morning away, happily exhausted, some probably just down from days on a ledge. Young European men—tan, unshaven, filthy and wearing filthy clothes—cooked coffee on little aluminum backpacking stoves next to their obligatory enormous American jalopies; men who'd lit out for a year, were taking time off. All over the lot were dusty old VW busses, outfitted with elaborate cabinets and beds, plastered with bumper stickers and window transparencies of stars, rainbows and the earth, of dancing acid bears and "Free Leonard Peltier." On the back of an old Ford van, a pharmacy's bumper sticker had been appropriated: "Wall Drug."

Nick and I got to work—he cooked up coffee while I organized the rack of protection the way Dad had shown me. When the coffee was ready we both shoved our hands in our Patagonia jacket pockets and unconsciously tried to look worn-out, like we'd almost killed ourselves the day before and needed a break. The sun over Half Dome branched down through the pines in broad, dusty rays. That these men were here at all, particularly the Europeans, the South Americans, the Japanese, meant they were in the midst of a lifetime dream—climbing in Yosemite Valley, in California, in America. World famous rock walls— El Capitan, Half Dome, Sentinel Rock, the Cathedral Group—some of the most compact, solid granite on earth.

While we nonchalantly laid our own gear out on the tailgate, we caught glimpses of guys' hands as they walked by: climbers' hands—swollen, coarse, soiled, covered with scabs from being shoved into cracks—real hands like my dad's, hands wrapped in white athletic tape as armor for the day's struggle. Two climbers who stood eating granola from tin cups were so lean and sunburnt they looked wolfish and undernourished. Definitely not studying postmodernism at Yale. They had adaptive body-types, wiry, tight and hard. My own hands seemed soft and intact.

Nick practiced coiling our new ropes on the ground. Embarrassingly clean, they were bright yellow with snake patterns of red and blue. Dad didn't mind my using his rack of chocks and Friends, but ropes were taboo. You never lent out ropes. Because they were kernmantles, with an elastic core sheathed in woven nylon, the core could be damaged without visible sign. The carabiners—aluminum ovals that fit perfectly between fingers and palm—each got an affectionate snap with the thumb; just practicing, getting a feel for them. Nick pulled the triggers on the Friends, added a little silicone dry-lube.

"Gears a little stiff?" I asked.

"Yeah," he said, from the back of his throat. "Little stiff."

He bit his upper lip and tried to look fierce as he thrust a Friend into the joint of my camper shell's door—pretending it was an overhead crack. Two tan, dreadlocked white guys kicked around a footbag in a patch of sunlight. They both had climbers' hands and sun-bleached beards. One had scratches across his chest and back and was so gaunt he'd tied his tattered canvas pants up with a string. His muscles flickered under his skin like woven piano wire. They kept the little leather bag in the air: warming up, talking about whether they should go down to the Cookie Cliff and try Butterfingers.

I grabbed our copy of the *Yosemite Climbs* guide book. The Cookie . . . Butterfingers . . . 5.11c. 5.11c! On a difficulty scale from 5.0 to 5.14, where 5.0 is virtually a steep staircase and 5.14 is an overhanging Teflon-coated mirror, 5.10 even seemed so thin as to be almost unclimbable. But 5.11c? And they couldn't have been much older than us . . . in fact a sharp-eyed blond kid looked younger. My Dad still hadn't led anything harder than 5.10. Climbing at that level had to be some kind of near-mystical dance, way out west, way up on walls. The picture of Butterfingers in the book looked like a perfect crack on a smooth, dead vertical wall. It looked like fingertips would fit inside, but not well.

On a broad green tarp by a camouflaged van a short, skinny guy with a long handlebar mustache and ponytail had spread out more gear than I'd ever seen. Nick poured us each another cup of coffee. Then he started putting our gear into our bright new packs while I snuck a few glances—a monstrous white bag stood off to the short guy's side, and I was sure it meant something. Although empty, it stood upright, about three feet high and cylindrical. Heavy nylon flatcord—or webbing—had been sewn down two sides, under the bottom and up again, forming thick loops above the open top of the bag.

Then it struck me—a haul bag. A real, Fish brand haul bag. The genuine article like Dad and Sean must have used on Half Dome. I'd seen pictures of them, and knew they were the only bags durable enough for hauling food and supplies up the great walls on multi-day climbs. Fish was rumored to have tested them by tying them to the back of his motorcycle and driving out on highways for hours at a time. This man was preparing for a big wall—a Big Wall— Half Dome, maybe even El Capitan, "The Captain," sleeping on ledges thousands of feet off the ground, doing nothing but climbing from dawn until dark, popping open a can of cold beans for dinner and having it taste better than any steak on the ground. A psychotic divorce from the world, requiring clarity of mind through long periods of terrifying quiet. My father had many books about Big Walls, photographs from his recent Half Dome climb.

Iron spikes called pitons were spread out all around the hero. Twenty or thirty soda bottles wrapped in duct tape stood empty against the red van—water for a week. I couldn't believe it. I had to stare, look at him closely, try to get some hint of how he could be so calm on the docks before sailing. His hands were already taped. It seemed such a bizarre aspiration, such an insane way to spend one's time without even the comfort of a beer in the meadow at day's end.

A strung-out redhead sat on the ground next to the Big Wall astronaut. He was tense and big-jawed. His wiry hair stuck out on all sides while he chattered away. He had his own pile of equipment.

"All for sale," he said to us, smiling with brown teeth, "all of it. Forty-three carabiners, a full free-climbing rack, ropes, slings, a few bugaboo pitons and five or six copperheads. Getting out of climbing."

"Why?"

"My buddy was fully soloing the DNB, like a few days ago, and I was watching him through the binocs when one of his hands just popped off, like a hold broke or something." He pursed his peeling lips and shook his head. "And I seriously saw him falling. I ran to the base of the cliff and his ankles were up in his hips. I freaked and jammed off for the medics. Those Friends are going for twenty bucks each."

Ten

Nick pulled khaki shorts over his tan legs and put on a pair of old New Balance running shoes. He took off his polo shirt just long enough to fish out and quickly pull on a white T-shirt—he was never too into people seeing his body. He slammed the tailgate shut and we bounced the truck over potholes and out of the lot. Off to a two-pitch route called Positively Fourth Street to practice lead climbing.

An hour getting organized. Then, absolutely covered with 'biners, stoppers, hexes and Friends, rock shoes on, harness buckled, chalkbag full, I grabbed the edge of a lieback flake, pulled up about six feet, felt my hands starting to sweat, and greased off. I landed hard on my feet and stumbled over backwards into a bush. I lay for a moment with a branch in my mouth trying to breathe, then rolled over so I could stand up with all the gear. I handed Nick the rack, untied from the rope, and said, "Hell with it. Your turn."

He looked away, shook his head, and said something I couldn't hear. I didn't ask him to repeat it, and after a min-

ute of looking into the forest and running his fingers
through his hair, he laced up his climbing shoes. It took
him a while to get them tight enough on his narrow feet. Up
off the ground, he started shoving gear into the crack about
every two feet, and I didn't blame him. Who knew if that
stuff would hold. And who wanted to find out.

"You watching me?!" he yelled.

"What do you think? I got you on belay."

"Watch me!" Was this narcissism or paranoia? I could
see veins standing out on his forearms and his left leg was
pumping in a spasm as regular as a sewing machine. If he
peeled I was going to get yanked.

"Watch me!" He was growling through clenched teeth,
his whole body locked in an awkward contortion.

"Dude . . . " I mumbled, getting worried.

"Shut up, shitfucker, I'm there." Suddenly he pulled
higher and stopped.

"Where?"

"The belay. The anchor." I climbed up quietly, shaking
my head. Not feeling too randy.

"What?" he said. "You're leading the next pitch, aren't
you?" He sounded slightly hysterical.

A corner led fifteen feet up to an overhang, and my
hands bled in the crack as I thrashed toward it. Hanging by
a hand jammed behind a flake, I could see chalk marks
leading left beneath the roof.

"How's it look?" Nick asked, squinting under his pre-
faded blue cap. I'd have to climb to the left underneath a
huge block by shoving my hands in a horizontal crack

behind it. My feet were melting in my dad's lousy, too-tight shoes. I scrambled out a little ways under the roof and shoved in a Friend. At first it wouldn't fit and my arms burned while I fought with it. Then back right to the corner. Panting, shaking out the forearms. Then, back left a little farther, another Friend. If I flew from underneath I risked slamming back into the corner.

Back out, past the first Friend, feet slipping around on the smooth granite, neck crammed up under the roof. Past the second Friend and the backs of my hands were getting slippery with blood. I grabbed the outside lip of the roof and was hanging way over backwards out in space no longer breathing and sweat stinging my eyes. My right hand shot over the roof and slapped onto a huge, solid handhold. One pull and I was over. Shrieking. Laughing while Nick looked about in embarrassment to make sure nobody'd heard me.

"Could do two more pitches," I said. "Looks casual in the guidebook."

Nick sat above the roof with me looking down at the ground.

"You sure?" he asked. "Shouldn't we just rappel down?" We were well above the treetops, and they were tall trees. "Seems kind of late," he said, "doesn't it? But on the other hand, I mean, rappeling could take a while. We're not real good at it." He took the red bandana off his neck—a ridiculous place for it—and put it in his shorts pocket. I racked up without asking any more questions. He got me on belay and I led off. As I climbed above he looked at his watch. The sun did seem low. For nearly two hours I led up dirt-filled cracks that probably hadn't been climbed in ten years. Soil fell in my eyes as I reached overhead for handholds. Nick periodically shook out his hair.

"You sure this is a route?" he yelled.

"Absolutely not."

"Beauty."

Above a wide ledge covered with loose rocks, I stumbled up a tree-filled gully, but right at nightfall it ran out in a blank wall. Nick followed up and we stood together in the darkness getting nervous. We weren't really sure what would happen on a cliff at night, hadn't even thought about it.

"What the hell?" Nick asked, apparently expecting an explanation.

"Be stupid to climb in the dark," I said. I wished I could see his face. "Don't you think?"

I looked overhead at the wall, now just a blacker part of the sky, then down below at a tiny pair of car headlights. Probably someone on their way to a steak dinner, maybe a couple with a nice hotel room. Nick leaned against a tree growing from the cliff and looked toward his feet.

"You didn't bring any pants or thermals?" he asked.

"No. You neither."

"Nope. We also spaced food and water. And rain gear. And matches."

"You know anything about hypothermia?"

"Just that you start feeling tired and wonderful right before you die."

"Guess it's you and me, then, huh?"

"What?"

"Spoons. You know . . . "

Nick shook his head and peered at his hands in the dark. Then said, "Better to be homosocial than dead, eh?"

"Much."

After a few minutes of getting used to the idea, he turned around and lay down in the dirt. I pressed my chest against his back, my legs against the backs of his. I felt him shiver. Half-asleep I hallucinated of rescues, of smiling competent men calling to me from a few yards away. A storm—or even a cold snap—would have killed us very quickly. I started awake once, hyperventilating and shaking, and noticed that a huge swath of stars was missing from the sky. Through the tree branches I could make out another amorphous vacant patch over the Cathedral group. A colder breeze sifted through the still warm valley air and a few leaves rustled.

I pressed myself closer to Nick's back and felt him shake from his stomach outward. He had wrapped one of the ropes around his upper body and had his cotton cap pulled low down over his ears. The flat tapping sound of light rain brushed across the tree and onto the wall nearby. I heard Nick say something.

"Hm?" I asked.

"I said this is bullshit."

I could have sworn there was a hint of accusation in his voice. Another patter came harder and a cold drop made it through the leaves onto my arm.

In the shadowless light before dawn I woke up, surprised to find I'd slept. Nick was wide awake and shaking all over. The whole sky was overcast and the cloud cover seemed to be lowering. When I sat up he looked at me for a moment, then asked sheepishly if we could go down now. The first three rappels (sliding down ropes hung from an anchor) to the last ledge—still a hundred feet off the ground—went quickly. We were both surprised by how much technique we'd picked up.

"If the sky dumps on us," I said, "we're screwed."

"You're right," Nick responded. "Once again, Dan's correct." Nick finally touched down on the ground and hooted up that he was off the rope. My bicep cramped as I pulled the rope into my rappel device. I had to stop for a moment to stretch it out—useless, untrained, collegiate muscles. I was leaning backward off the ledge when I noticed a dark curtain of rain moving down the valley toward us. Just as I swung back under the big overhang the curtain hit and I was soaked and shivering in seconds. The wall instantly became a light waterfall; my feet slipped against the rock and the rope became slick and hard to hang onto. Dirt and water poured over my braking fist and down my limbs. My T-shirt clung cold against my back while a wind blew me to one side.

Then I was down. My feet were on talus and I was shaking in big convulsions. Water squirted out the lace-holes of my suede climbing shoes. Nick helped me get free of the rope then pulled it down from the anchor. I clipped all the scattered gear onto my harness and chest rack while Nick wrapped the ropes in a mess of knots and coils around his shoulders. We ran stiffly through the forest back to the car. Inside, finally warming up, we drove over to Yosemite's grand Ahwahnee Hotel where Queen Elizabeth once stayed. Feeling a little stupid, we walked under the massive redwood beams of the vaulted hall and past leather couches and cozy fires. Still filthy and freaked out, we stepped into the formal dining room and grabbed a couple of mimosas. Then we loaded green china plates with smoked trout at the all-you-can-eat buffet. At a steam table of eggs Benedict, Nick stopped and looked at me, suddenly exasperated.

"You enjoyed that," he said.

"I don't know."

"There's something very, very wrong with that."

Eleven

Plumb out of yang, no desire to get to the top of anything, I mulled over how to break it to Nick. Over a plate of bad French toast at the Yosemite cafeteria, I remembered Kyla'd be back from the music festival by now, converted or not.

"Dan," he said, before I could open my mouth, "I can't do it. I'm just not in the right space to climb." We were in the car and on the road back home with more coffee, and Nick was rubbing the muscles of his neck with both hands and talking about how much the storm had shaken him. Really gotten under his skin. The confession came pouring out; he needed me to know he wasn't like me, whatever that meant. He didn't get off on death. "I mean," he said, "I gotta think this through some more. Be a shame to die just to impress my mom."

We passed the park entrance where a row of cars a half mile long waited to pay entrance fees. Enormous RVs with names like High Plains Drifter and Footloose had canoes strapped to their roofs and Suzuki 4x4s in tow. Nick took off his glasses, breathed on a lens, wrapped his shirt around

it and started kneading with his fingers. He told me he'd en-
rolled in a figure painting class at the university. I crassly
asked if the nude models had anything to do with it.

"You do have the mind of a five-year-old after all," he
responded. "But frankly, the teacher, this French lady, is
unbelievable." He put his foot out the window in the breeze
and I wished I could do the same. "My mother's not going
to believe it," he said. "She hates it when I change obses-
sions too quickly."

Twelve

After a long, meandering drive out to Point Reyes, carsick from apple-strawberry juice and fig bars, Kyla and I parked in an empty dirt lot near a dairy farm. We put on warm clothes and walked out through sheep and cattle pasture toward the fogbound beach of Abbots Lagoon. I rambled for a while about my epic with Nick and how he'd apparently had some kind of mental break over the whole subject, but I couldn't quite find the right tenor for the story—was I thrilled by the danger? Exaggerating it to impress her? Contemptuous of Nick or supportive? She didn't seem sure on any count, and I realized I wasn't either. So I asked about the women's music festival. Tried to keep my voice neutral, not sound mercenary.

"Overwhelming," she said. She pulled her arms into the body of her thick fisherman's sweater and let the sleeves swing around as she walked.

"How? In a bad way?"

"Yeah . . . sort of." She looked at me with wide eyes. " I thought it'd be different with women. Not such a pickup scene, but it was totally the same." She got an arm free and pointed suddenly—an egret stood in the reeds of the lagoon like a white flamingo in a northern garden. Its long neck arched with an elegance contrived and almost un-Darwinian. Friends had warned her that the Yosemite festival was notorious, that it probably wasn't the best place to look into being with women.

"Look," she said, sounding very frank, "the whole thing with me wanting to be with women was just that men weren't making me happy. Or not the ones I'd been with, anyway. I've had fun sex with men, but only a couple of times."

And where does that leave me, I wondered. Sure, like most guys I secretly fancied myself an artful, healing lover, but this could be quite a burden. Men, she said, just never bothered to find out what felt good for her; her mind usually wandered to phone bills or to imagining what her body would look like from above. She poured wet sand into circles as she talked. A leather thong around her ankle was encrusted with salt from walking in the surf.

"I'd really decided not to be with men at all anymore," she said. "You should know that."

The past-perfect verb tense was a tip-off . . . she was open to a change of mind. She drew a finger along the lovely downy hair above her lip. Again I wanted to kiss her, to just get past this nutty talk. I mean, here we were! On a deserted beach! But instead, I said, "Why should I know that?"

She took my left hand and held it for a moment. She started to pick at the scab of a climbing cut, then leaned forward in the sand and, without looking at me, put her arms around me. I hugged back, firmly but without any idea what it meant. I could smell the wool of her sweater and some oil she was wearing; far down the beach a person slipped in and out of my range of vision—a shimmering little stick figure in the sand.

"Can I kiss you?" I asked.

"Yes."

She kept her eyes open and put her closed mouth softly against mine, then turned and walked on.

Later, we were sitting with our backs against a driftwood log watching the undertow when she smiled to herself.

"What?" I asked.

"I had this thought," she said. "I just sort of pictured us taking off all our clothes." I kept looking at the ocean.

"You mean . . . to swim?" I asked, still looking at the ocean.

"Yeah, or whatever."

"Do you . . . do you want to?"

"What, swim? Or take my clothes off?"

"Either."

I found myself sitting in the fog, a wet wind blowing from the north, naked. But how to sit, naked? Akimbo, and I'd feel exposed. Slouched back on my elbow, and not only would I feel preposterous, but I'd freeze. I put my arms around my knees and looked at Kyla. She sat akimbo with her back straight and reached her arms up to the sky; goosebumps spread across her breasts. She smiled just a little, without implication, and looked at the surface of my eyes. Her body looked strong and beautiful, and I thanked God I was too cold to embarrass myself. As I shifted my chilled butt a little in the fine white sand I wondered whether it was even OK to think such things, or if she was counting on me to stay neutered in platonic hyperspace.

T h i r t e e n

On the road back from Abbots Lagoon, through the bram-
bles and dense coastal forests around Inverness, I asked
Kyla if she had to be back in town for any reason. Some
journalist friends of my parents owned a farmhouse nearby,
and they'd offered it to me more than once. She seemed
happy to stretch out the trip, didn't appear to want to go
home anytime soon, so we made the drive a little farther
north to the mouth of a small bay. A huge, rambling old
white Victorian, the house was bordered on three sides by
sheep range. Their caretaker, an old Marxist painter, lived
out back in a chicken coop full of artifacts of the Revolution and Chinese miniature houses inhabited by dried,
dressed-up cockroaches. When I knocked on his flimsy
screen door I could see a paintbrush and sickle hanging
over the stove. The bent, red-faced and charismatic old
man recognized me from a family picnic and let us into the
main house.

"Could you live like this?" Kyla asked, over a pot of tea
in the big country kitchen. "In the country, I mean. Grow
food, hang out?" I looked around at all the great copper

pots hanging over the cooking range, at the early American furniture, the brick barbecue outside and the misty green hillsides; I imagined shacking up with Kyla in a place like this, opening a bed and breakfast, maybe trying to write a novel. I told her yeah, I thought so, but it would really help if there was a surf break or a climbing area nearby so I wouldn't lose my mind. She rolled her eyes and started rubbing butter into flour for a pie crust. "I could do this forever," she said. "Little garden out back? This is pretty much heaven to me."

We cooked for hours—lentil dahl, tangerine chutney and a peach pie—but I had to drink the cabernet alone. Kyla wasn't in the mood for red wine and it brought back my last college girlfriend again—she'd actually had a red wine fetish, something about all the implied late nights and worldly sadness, some ridiculous earthiness we'd affected together but wouldn't own. Kyla's triceps stood out in the soft kerosene light while she dried the dishes I'd just washed.

That night we slept in an attic room, and when I blew out the kerosene lantern the light from the Presbyterian church steeple spilled white across the bed. Kyla seemed to like being touched, and I stayed well within the implied non-aggression pact. Eventually I stopped moving my hand and settled back into the sheets. After a moment, she touched back, lightly, though she watched her hands on my skin as if watching a pigeon eat birdseed. Soon I fell asleep.

Fog pushed over hills on the sheep range where we walked the next morning and I listened as Kyla told me about more crummy relationships, some bastard boyfriend who'd date-raped her. We lay for a few hours next to an overturned car and watched sheep ambling around, lambs suckling. I took a good look at this woman I was following around, at the pleasure she took in exactly the places I'd been dying to come home to. She'd never left them and didn't want to; she didn't seem at all programmed with the lemminglike American impulse to flee home.

Back at the house, I started throwing a tennis ball for a lunatic border collie. The Episcopal service let out and families lingered by the side of the green, foggy sheep pastures to talk to the minister. The rancher who owned the dog walked over to introduce himself. He had huge forearms.

"I'd offer you my hand," I said, "but it's covered with dog spit."

He laughed and smiled. He was a wiry man.

"I've had my hands up inside sheep all morning," he said proudly, "didn't have time to wash them. We've been lambing."

Kyla mentioned how cute the lambs had been out in the fields, wandering around on their loose little legs. I agreed.

"Been a problem this year with the ravens," the rancher explained, suddenly dour, "flying in when the ewe's not looking and plucking the lamb's anus and pulling their intestines out. The lambs are still alive when we get there and they just look up at you, wondering what to do. It's awful."

We stopped at the Calistoga Fair on the way back to Berkeley and Kyla spent an hour picking through rummage tables; a terrific haul, sheer booty—five wooden spoons and three wooden bowls, all for a song.

Fourteen

Redwood shelves reached from floor to ceiling in the den of my family's little green Victorian in Berkeley. The first two were all records, old-time bluegrass and eccentric folk music: *The Seldom Scene, Act Two, Snake Baked a Hoe Cake, Music of the Poison Coyote Kid, Dawg Music*. The upper shelves were British and American poetry while the middle held the prescient material: *Savage Arena*—"A gripping tale of tremendous courage and unbelievable endurance," *The Climb Up to Hell, Mountain of My Fear, Eiger, Wall of Death, The White Spider, Shining Mountain—Two Men on Changabang's West Wall, Everest the Hard Way, The Vertical World of Yosemite, Touching the Void*.

Dad uncorked a bottle of wine and poured three glasses at our round dinner table—an old San Francisco cable-car spool. Mom got back from her editing job in time to pull together polenta with a spicy tomato sauce and a spinach jicama salad. Before she sat down she pulled the curtains to block out the crumbling stucco tenement across the street. On one wall of our dining room hung a black-and-white photograph of a storefront in Ireland with the sign "Duane's Victuallers." No relation, but in the picture we all stood out front—Dad had long sideburns and a mustache. He wore a jeans jacket and cowboy boots. I was six years old and looked miserable. My sister was three and wore a dirty checked dress. Mom wore a dark turtle-necked sweater and was the only one in the picture who was smiling.

I poured a second glass of wine while Dad told me about climbing he'd done down in Joshua Tree. Mom had already heard the whole story, but took off her work shoes and listened anyway to how he climbed mornings but spent afternoons alone in the desert. "I didn't tell you, though," he said to Mom, "how I went into that biker bar one night. Just minding my own business when all these Angels and Air Force guys turn around staring at me." My sister was off at college in Oregon, so Dad was indulging in more climbing talk than usual.

"Well," he continued, "I had to take a leak so I got up and walked into the bathroom. I was about to wash my hands when I looked in the mirror and understood. At age fifty, there I was, a lawyer with kids, bald and filthy with half a beard, scabs all over my head, my lips burned-out and chapped, my clothes soiled and shredded and my hands not only entirely wrapped in white tape but covered with bloodstains. Like a serial killer."

He loved it. Mom shook her head and walked into the kitchen. She'd heard variations on the theme for a long time, the guy who poses as a lawyer just to pay the bills but actually, in his heart of hearts, lives for wild times in the

American outback. I think she liked the idea—I know I did—and it was partly a shared vision; they'd spent their first few years together and even given birth to me while living in a VW bus. Not playing hippy, either, but doing civil rights legal work in the South of the 1960s. She also didn't mind his leaving to climb all the time. It gave her space, kept things fresh.

"The weirdest part," Dad said, "was this climber's party at a trailer home. The guy had life figured out—taught grammar school right in J-Tree: afternoons off to climb, vacations, low rent. Kooky though, because all over the walls he had pictures of breasts matched up with pictures of mountains."

Dad and I left that night for Yosemite right after dinner. The Nutcracker Suite, he told me on the long drive up, was the best 5.8 grade climb in Yosemite. We were awake the next morning by 5:30 a.m. and walking to its base by 7:00 a.m. I ate a dry piece of sourdough bread as we approached. Mist hung low over the grass and the ground below the rock had been trampled into hard, barren dirt. The granite of Manure Pile Buttress curved up out of sight.

"Beautiful route, Danny," he said. "A classic. Jesus, I'm glad to be here. All right . . . harness is doubled-back, my knot looks good. Got to do this. You always get the other guy to check your knot and harness. You look good. Check mine."

He made the first fifteen feet easily, placed a stopper and clipped the rope to it. I heard voices. Two men wearing red helmets appeared.

"I don't believe it," one said when he saw us. He looked at his watch and dropped his pack. Dad had another stopper in farther up. His fingers were inside the crack while his feet moved around on the smoother granite below.

"Watch me, son," he said, "little crux here." My brake hand tightened. If he fell and the top stopper popped, he'd have a shot at cratering. But he'd done the route before and seemed loose and focused. He shifted his feet for purchase, then slotted his right hand high in the crack. I heard one of the guys mumble that the move looked desperate.

"Guy's just making it look hard," his friend said. "I've done it a million times. We're going to hit waaaaaay worse on Half Dome, my friend." The guy said "Half Dome" a little loud, like I was supposed to take note that they were heavies.

Ten feet more and Dad was at a ledge; sun had moved down to just above where he sat. He took off his blue sweatshirt before getting me on belay. The forest had warmed up and mosquitos came out. I followed, and Dad led the next two pitches without a problem; he was setting an anchor beneath a roof when the latecomers appeared on the big ledge where I was sitting.

I finally got a good look at the leader—he reminded me of certain guys who showed up at the Berkeley bouldering area on weekends: old canvas climbing pants, a tan flannel shirt—a nonfunctional, cultivated look. His boots were early Royal Robbins—obsolete, but the badge of an old-timer. He'd banged up his helmet over the years and, with his sandy beard, it hid most of his face.

I looked over at the Cathedral group directly across the valley as he told his follower about the great old days when he'd climbed with Royal Robbins and Chuck Pratt. A minute later the guy squinted up at my father.

"Hey, what's he doing up there?" he said. "What the hell's taking so long?"

I said I didn't know. I thought he was just setting a safe anchor, and that was all right with me. I liked my dad's style on the life and death issue.

"For crying out loud," he said. Then he asked what other routes we were going to do. I said I thought Dad had mentioned the Braille Book.

"Bring an eleven hex," he said, "you'll need it." It sounded like he thought he'd given great advice, but since Dad had done the Braille Book a few times before, I decided not to pass it on. Dad looked down at me and I caught a little sardonic smile. He could hear everything.

The whole park's morning campfire smoke still hung in the trees. "We're going to have to climb through you guys," the old-timer said. "Yup. We can't just be waiting around for you." He leaned back to yell at Dad when I stopped him. Whatever Dad was doing, I was sure he had a reason.

"Actually," I said, "I think he'd really mind."

"Huh?"

"You yelling at him. He'd get pissed. Trust me." The truth was, he'd probably have just ignored them.

"Shit." He looked up-valley to Half Dome and Cloud's Rest. "You know," he said, "when Royal Robbins did the first ascent of this route we used to wear hiking boots on these climbs. It was all about ethics back then. In fact, this whole route was about ethics. When I climbed with Robbins, nuts instead of pitons was brand-new and we didn't have sticky shoes like you guys either. Your dad should be clipped in and gone. What the hell." He looked up again, squinting from under his helmet. "You guys ought to try some of the easy routes over on the apron." He shook his head, looking disgusted. "Not as crowded. On a route this crowded you got to move fast."

He went back to telling his partner about other famous guys he used to hang out with in Camp Four at these great big campfire bullshit sessions when there were only a handful of Yosemite climbers and they all knew each other. The Golden Years.

Dad yelled down that I could start climbing. It took me a few minutes to calm down enough, but then I pulled out our anchor and stepped off the ledge. Clean granite flakes formed a pathway of perfect holds and soon I was just doing it—moving.

An older man appeared on the ledge below from a different route. I heard him asking the belligerent if he couldn't just climb on through.

"No goddam way. I've done this route too many times. You're waiting. Period."

The newcomer said he was doing a different route, that he wouldn't get in the way at all. The grouch told him he had a few things to learn about etiquette, and that if he wanted to get up this thing without waiting he should've woken up earlier. The older man said one more time that he wouldn't be on the same route and the grouch's partner finally voted for giving in.

Within minutes the older climber was beneath me. He heard me calling up to Dad about the bad vibes below.

"Don't worry," the man said, "I'm not going to run you over. You guys are doing just fine. Lovely route, huh?" By the time I'd climbed another ten feet the man was past me and setting an anchor at a tree off to my left. My dad nodded to him and said into my ear, "What a coincidence, that's Royal Robbins."

F i f t e e n

South on freeways through the sunny smog corridor of the
East Bay—watched over by wild Ohlone hills and red-tailed
hawks still circling the highway in obsolete ancestral patterns. Around the southern tip of the San Francisco Bay
through sprawling, vacuous San Jose, then west among the
lush and rugged Santa Cruz Mountains and into Santa
Cruz: haunted Aquarian beach town on the north shore of
Monterey Bay. Kyla's last term in college—I followed her
down with a full load in my pickup. As we descended to the
coast a fog bank lingered out past the white-capped blue of
the bay.

Kyla's new roommates, Denise and Carmen, had
already organized the kitchen, arranged bins for communal
bulk foods. Kyla had filled my truck with boxes and boxes of
jars—countless little ones full of herbs, bigger ones of wal-
nuts, pine nuts, sesame seeds and poppy seeds; large ones
of buckwheat groats, whole wheat flour, basmati and jasmine rice, barley and pasta. With Denise's muscular, hair-
less boyfriend Keith, I shuttled boxes while the roommates
reunited on the front deck. Denise, by concentrating in

Colonial Diasporas, had effectively majored in self-loathing. A tense and beautiful dancer from Redding, she wore her blond hair in a tight bun. Clean Levis and clogs. Her posture arced up into a drawn longbow and she wanted absolutely all of the food shared; she insisted the three women cook dinner together twice a week.

"Without men," she said to Kyla, unaware I was listening.

Kyla winked at me, knowing I'd heard. Carmen bent over into yogic "down-facing dog" and spoke quickly. She asked that Friday and Saturday nights be "candles only," no electric lights. Kyla nodded with her eyes closed in the sun as I tottered under the weight of her queen-sized futon. At last in a household they could make perfect, they would work hard at the pleasures that brought them together—hand-mixed herbal teas (medicinal, uplifting, soothing, aphrodisiacal, digestive), homemade lip balms with beeswax and essential oils, skin salves, face masks; they baked bread immediately—full of grains, nuts, seeds and love—and took turns kneading. The bread kneaded back as if alive, drawing them a step closer to the ever-receding ideal of groundedness. They'd imagined a healing womanspace away from their boyfriends, away from cities and packaged foods and all forms of pollution, including the emotional.

I stood on a wooden chair and pinned dried flowers to Kyla's white plaster wall—she had garbage bags full of them and the sweet, dusty smell billowed out as I worked. Then Kyla put a finger to her lips and I froze—Denise screamed in her bedroom and a hand hit a wall. I heard her call Keith a fucker and the bedsprings squeaked. Keith, an art major minoring in bodywork, shouted back something about sensitivity and a moment later they came into the kitchen smiling. While Kyla and Carmen gulped green tea from ceramic and wooden bowls that warmed the hands, Denise and Keith brewed it in a one-cup Japanese teapot and drank from tiny ceremonial cups—a tablespoon at a time with long breaths in between.

Carmen had volunteered to run a discussion section on eating disorders for Feminism 1A; the class and the poet who taught it had become campuswide symbols of women's strength and self-empowerment. For her first project, Carmen planned to create a collection of photographs of women's bellies. So while I drank an iced mint sun tea and picked at my guitar, she and Kyla spent much of that first afternoon in the pale Mediterranean light of their home celebrating and photographing each other's bodies—their roundness and fullness, their perfect imperfection. They took rolls and rolls of film of one another nude on the redwood patio: meditative, vulnerable, powerful.

Sixteen

Kyla pulled a long suede jacket over her fisherman's sweater while I put the top down on the Ghia; it was a cold, clear fall evening, and we drove north of Santa Cruz to watch the sunset from an uncrowded beach. We parked on Route One and walked out a dirt road across railroad tracks and along a cliff over the ocean. A tractor sat in a just-harvested Brussels sprout field and below a layer of magenta clouds the sun washed the air over the water in a diffuse, pale gold. Purple and white foxtails, bright yellow wild mustard and green chamomile grew among the grass in the middle of the lane. A cormorant floated with an updraft above the cliffs.

"You ever been back East?" I asked. A rhetorical question, really.

"No. Why?"

"No reason." With the ludicrous romance of the scene—blue surf peeling across reefs and pounding into majestic cliffs, the hillsides orange with ripe pumpkins—I couldn't help but want to strip naked and make wild love in the wind, roll among the Brussels sprouts. Or at least just hug. But I didn't have Kyla figured out yet, and still couldn't predict her moods: there was some spark that hadn't quite flown for her yet, and a proposition risked proving I was just a horn-dogger after all.

We sat in the shelter of a storm-beaten old cypress that leaned away from the sea as if permanently bowing to a northwesterly wind. Smells of rotting kelp from the beach below, of the wave spray and of the bed of pine needles beneath us eddied about in the tree's shade. The Pacific horizon touched the ball of the sun in a clean tangent. I thought of leaning my head on her shoulder, or maybe holding her hand, but then wondered why I hesitated.

"Do you . . . " I thought over the phrasing, "just an open question. Not loaded. No right answer. But, do you . . . like me?"

She thought for a moment, wrinkling her lovely brow and picking at the bark of the cypress. Then she asked gently what I meant. The mass of her hair fell to one side as she looked up.

"I mean, no big deal," I stuttered, "just . . . do you . . . you know . . . sort of basically like my presence, more or less?"

"Are you kidding?"

"No."

"Why would I be sleeping with you and letting you practically live with me?"

"Fine. Ok, fine. You're perfectly right. Just tripping on how you never grab the back of my head and sock your tongue in my mouth. Just an example. Or even solicit hugs."

"Am I lacking something?" she asked. The question seemed weighted with déjà vu.

"Nothing. Absolutely nothing."

"Seems a little cold to have sex, doesn't it? I mean, we could." She looked around suddenly at the dirt and grass as if intrigued.

"Not at all what I was thinking about, but, hey, that's fine. Doesn't seem too cold to me, but that's fine. I'm warm-blooded."

"Well, I'm not," she admitted, taking my hand.

Under a natural bridge the size of L'Arc de Triomphe, seabirds had built nests in small holes vacated by falling rocks. Kyla picked up a long strand of kelp, and while she held it I popped its air sacs one by one. A lone surfer in a shining black wetsuit paddled farther outside; a big wave was building. I had just crushed another air sac when Kyla spoke to the sea.

"But I like being with you a lot," she said. She let go of the kelp so only I held it.

"Me?" I asked. I had no idea why I suddenly felt so insecure.

The surfer sat up and wheeled around to paddle with the wave. It jacked up behind him, a black wall at least twice his height.

"Yes. You." The top of the wave started to feather and spray. He pushed his shoulders up off the board with his hands. "It's not what I thought I was looking for," she said, "but it feels good right now." The wave below the surfer sucked out.

"You want to come climbing?" I asked.

"How about just backpacking first?" The surfer sprang to his feet, now perched on the heaving lip.

Seventeen

Heading out west from California's shores meant driving inland to the wild near east. Smoke-belching RVs had over-run stinking hot Yosemite Valley and lines had formed on all the classic climbs, so Nick and I lit out for Tuolumne Meadows. But up in that beautiful high country, daily thundershowers kept us off the rock and under the grill's awning, drinking beer and watching lightning pop on the domes. A good life, for a while, but I started getting antsy. A skinny blond guy with thick glasses and shredded pink knee pants told us about climbs out east in a river gorge without a river, over in the desert on the eastern side of the Sierra. Nick sprinted through a flash hailstorm into the grocery store while I started the truck.

In fifteen minutes, with a bag of tortilla chips and a couple of ice cream sandwiches, we'd left white domes and evergreen forests and were dropping into the Great Basin. The high landscape of white and green gave way to one dry and wide open; horizons of pale bronze and dull browns. Below the old Tioga Pass Resort the highway cut along a huge rocky drainage out of the Sierra, and we looked east across the moonscape of Mono Basin, past the volcanic Aeolian Buttes and far into the Nevada ranges beyond.

"Come on, dude," I said, "why won't you tell me about that French painting teacher?"

Nick took off his glasses and looked at himself in them, then put them back on and pulled my rearview mirror around.

"Honestly," I said, "I'm just curious."

"I know you are. Why're you such a punk about this kind of stuff?" he said. "And what about this Kyla person? Isn't she a little . . . how you say . . . mystical?"

"I'm working on it," I said. "She's meeting me up here in a week."

"Kind of sprung on her, huh?"

"Yeah. I'm a little sprung."

Nick, shy as he was, managed constant, back-to-back flings with knockouts; women doomed to chase brooding recalcitrance. But it killed him that he could never make it last longer than two weeks; he always got bored, or scared that they were. His mom, prematurely anxious about her prospects for grandchildren, had begun giving him books on male-female communication.

Looking west from the western slope, we'd have seen forested hills petering out into the Central Valley, maybe the coastal range beyond, covered with dry, yellow grass. Like looking back east into the Hudson Valley from the Catskills two hundred years ago—west would have been the way home, the way back to the settled lands. East from Tioga pass, at least for Nick and me, was more like gazing into the territories.

At the bottom of the pass we turned right and drove

south on 395, parallel to the whole ragged range. Big thunderstorms still darkened much of the Sierra Crest, and we occasionally saw little silent flashes and bolts of lightning. Past Deadman's Summit, the jagged Minarets rose like black skeletal fingers behind the broad flanks of Mammoth Mountain; farther, the awesome buttress of Mount Morrison loomed dark over the highway. Past Convict Lake the Long Valley spread out to drop into the Owens Valley; to the east the White Mountains stood dry. In Dad's office I'd seen Daliesque photographs of the Whites, of pink sunset snowscapes and gnarled thousand-year-old bristlecone pines.

"My teacher's an idiot," Nick said. We passed a green church standing alone in the sage. "And I'm a bigger idiot." His hair had grown out a little, and he'd been keeping it under the light blue cap. He rolled down a window and the air had a static-electric aridity infused with the sweet, spicy smell of desert sage.

A few pathetic houseboats drifted on the vast, shallow puddle that was Crowley Lake, and when we stopped at the general store for water I had to sneak into the crummy little bathroom to fill up because the cashier was feeling stingy. In the front seat of a parked camouflage-painted Land Rover a border collie looked at me with driven, pale blue eyes. In the back of the vehicle a leather-hooded falcon fidgeted.

Farther south we made a U-turn around an orange Cal-trans maintenance station and pulled onto the dirt Gorge Road. Heading due east away from the highway, we rattled along on the washboard surface, coins hopping off the dashboard and dust covering our glasses. Out the dusty windshield we had a jiggling view across sage again to those barren White Mountains. A view of drought, broken by a gleaming steel pipeline: the Owens River. An elevated cylinder laid over cracked dirt channelled the spring runoff of two mountain ranges to Los Angeles, parallel to the path the water had once carved in the desert.

We stepped out of the truck at a gravel turnout by a gate and Nick coughed in the cloud of dirt. I had to wipe off my glasses before I could see anything. There was broken glass everywhere—some from beer bottles, some from car windows. The gorge lay only a few yards away, and we stepped over to look down. No real transition marked the place; hard pale dirt just dropped to slopes of pumice blocks, all very loose. A hundred feet down, the sandy-brown pumice ended in steep cliffs of dark brown basalt. Entirely absent were the contrasts that define place in less tampered-with systems. Without a river, the attendant rushing of air and water remained an implication. A place worn into the desert floor by spring mountain runoff should have bubbled with cool pools and green life. Instead, desert sun bleached scrub grass to the palor of the mineral background. Beyond the locked gate, past a sign saying "Property of the Los Angeles Department of Water and Power," an asphalt road led down into the gorge.

Sitting on the tailgate in the heat, I licked chocolate mess from my ice cream wrapper. I could actually feel my skin starting to burn, and I pulled a strip off my nose. Nick drank lukewarm water from a duct-taped plastic Coke bottle. A dark sedan trailed a cloud of dust a half-mile off in the sage. Nick's hands were scabbed over—a little more like proper climber's hands—and he had sharp tan lines around the straps of his nylon sandals.

When it got too hot to sit, we packed up our gear and walked the road's clean blacktop into the gorge; pastel chunks of pumice lay out in the shiny, tar-black lane. Our feet shuffled on the pavement and echoed across the gorge. We stopped once, and for an instant could hear ourselves walking. Nick shuffled again, then stopped again. Then he yelled into the gorge, but only his own words came back—as frustrating as one's perfect reflection in a puddle. At least a running stream warps your face back with a foreign ripple, suggesting dialogue with the world. The sun was below zenith, and down in the gorge's shadow we stayed out of day and dead heat.

I told Nick how in the woods back East I never got over how every hill hid another like it, or another gulch or gentle rise—backroads and backwoods, little creeks and dense deciduous forest. Granted, history was in the dirt, but I couldn't get oriented.

The San Francisco Bay had big visual cues: the Berkeley Hills opposite the Golden Gate; the San Francisco Peninsula stretching south to Santa Cruz; Marin and Mount Tam beginning the headlands of northern California. Route 395 had had the same effect that day—the whole Sierra Nevada just off to the west while the Mono Basin dropped through valleys to the Mojave Desert. Ranges to the east rippled clear through the Great Basin to the Rockies.

Nick pulled our photocopied guidebook from my pack. We stood on the asphalt and looked around—the steep brown walls were pockmarked with sharp edges, pockets, splotches of white climber's chalk. The routes themselves, because they ascended no particular mountains or even to the tops of the cliffs, were delineated only by vertical lines of shiny steel expansion bolts. Just a "place" where someone drilled a row of holes. Visually, they were so homogeneous that their names seemed absurdly unrelated to the climbs—Guns and Poses, Funky Cole Patina, Rim Job, Fear of a Black Planet.

As we worked our way from route to route, belaying out of the old river bottom, hiding out in the shade from the sun, we both felt a vague paranoia. Building a road and drilling bolts took a lot of humans, and there were none around. The climbs were hard and short, requiring long reaches and powerful technique. Without a summit, we focused instead on linking technically difficult moves. Nick excelled—he had a powerful grace and, if nobody else was watching, could stay focused and calm at the brink of his strength. With no need to place gear for protection, we just clipped the rope into the pre-placed bolts—danger had been worked out of the system like predators out of the backcountry. The rock became a natural gymnasium. This freedom from responsibility, from commitment, and mainly from spectators freed Nick to dance, and he quickly out-climbed me.

And the rock wore down my fingertips, strained my tendons. I fell repeatedly and my harness cut into my raw, sweating hips. My eyes burned from dripping sweat; dust clung to my back and tickled my throat; cramped climbing shoes heated my feet. The ropes picked up so much dirt below every route that soon our hands and clothes were filthy. After a few routes, we moved on—searching cliffs to locate more routes. Their names in the book felt like a kind of perverse language projected onto the walls: Bow Down to the Standard White Jesus, Flush Twice—L.A. Needs the Water. A few beautiful names made us pause and look, as if that patch of rock might somehow be different—Conquistadors without Swords, Transcendance. Others befouled any vestigial fantasy we may have had of wild purity—Me So Horny, Show Us Your Tits, Black Chicks in Heat. At a widening in the gorge an old hydroelectric plant straddled the riverbed; rockslides had smashed its roof, and the windows had long since been broken. Cement sloughs ran under the plant on both sides. Nick jumped up onto a pumice boulder and yelled suddenly.

"Hey!" It echoed away to the south around the bends of the canyon.

The remnants of this first wringing-out of the gorge seemed less damaging than the glistening pipeline up above; the sloughs and wells at least connoted the presence of water; and their ruined state had the quality of Renaissance paintings in which peasants gather at crumbling aqueducts—a comforting entropy in the panicked development of the West.

Exhausted, we shouldered our now broken-in packs and walked farther up the gorge for a place to have lunch.

Around a bend, beneath two-hundred-foot towers of basalt, the pavement ended in a brand-new, tar-sticky black parking lot. Behind a high chain-link fence stood an enormous, humming power plant—converters and coils with the same sheen as the pipeline above. The river here had been run down through turbines and then back up out of the gorge. A single set of wires shot over the chain-link fence, through one relay tower, and out to the highway.

Iron bars and cement buttressing reinforced the cliffs over the plant; stenciled numbers on the natural stone walls tracked the shifting of truck-sized blocks. A white Ford pickup sat gleaming in the sun and a tired old German shepherd beneath it watched us pass. Out of sight and earshot of the plant, the gorge quieted down. We kicked pebbles and dust, hopped from pumice boulder to basalt boulder and meandered down the sandy riverbed in the gorge's hollow corridor. At a bend, the length of the gorge framed the Owens Valley beyond. Flat desert light and the consistency of hue obscured depth; elements of landscape—gorge walls, mountains, sky—all appeared a two-dimensional collage. A breeze cooled my neck just before the sun struck us hard. Within moments my bare, freckled arms felt hotter and my neck burned. Nick took off his cap and wiped his forehead.

The gorge widened as we wandered and house-sized brown blocks stood free of the main cliffs. Even larger ruins filled the riverbed; another big neoclassical WPA plant looked as if it had been hit by mortar rounds. We picked our way up loose masonry walls; a wooden toilet stall lay against a steel gate. Holes in the floor exposed dark wells where the turbines had been. No vines overtook the ruin and split its walls, no grass grew up through its floors or flowers over the roof. Walls waited for another rockslide to weaken them, windows waited for vandals. No spiders webbed over the doorways, no birds nested in the eaves. The building just got wet in the rain, then dried off, froze a bit in the winter, then thawed. The only erosion came with the wind, the only movement from tumbling pumice.

Back among the towers, looking for a climb called Sendero Luminoso, I felt my exhaustion. My worn-out arms hung heavy with blood and my fingertips were sore to the touch. Flush out of aggression. I sat against a block and breathed while Nick uncoiled the rope. Such a long, unchanging day without weather or wind, dawn or dusk. An iron loop rusted in a little block before me.

Nick placed a Friend at head height and clipped the rope to it, tried to muster the energy for a last route. He pulled up on the first holds, got his feet up off the ground, and started to sweat. His right foot slipped an inch, then jerked back into place. He slapped around overhead looking for a hold, and I saw his face wake up from the sleep we'd both been walking in. Then the rock under his right foot crumbled. I locked the belay brake as he lurched backwards but the Friend burst through loose rock. Nick took a mouthful of basalt, turned his ankle, and tumbled into dry weeds. Dazed, he lay for a while spitting. I untied from the rope and watched a lizard do push-ups.

Nick took off his shoes and sat for a long time in the dirt. He rubbed between his dirt-caked toes and picked at a toenail. After a while he stood up, shook the dust out of his hair and coiled the ropes. As we walked back through the gorge I felt contained: no marine air, limited perspective. Cliffs low enough so that the gorge felt like only half the relevant picture, never quite a place itself—and no summits, nowhere to get to. Around each bend we walked under distinct fracture patterns, rosette and spiral crystallization on a macro scale. Clarity of sky connected the walls. The sun's hot light hinted at great space outside the gorge. Without wind, traffic, crunch of the forest floor or the rush of water one realizes the quiet of the sun—it explodes silently.

Where the road rose back up the gorge wall, the Ford pickup from the power plant stopped to give us a ride. The mustached driver just motioned for us to jump in back with the dog; perhaps with all our gear we seemed more akin to engineers than hated environmentalists. As we got in, a dark cloud slipped under the sun. By the time we'd emerged onto the open plain we could see that an afternoon storm had already spread down from the high country. We hopped out and as the pickup drove off the dog watched us from the back. Winds swept the high desert and big drops smacked into the dirt. Clouds and rain engulfed a peak far up in the Sierra. The Buttermilks looked desolate and wet, putting afternoon bouldering out of the question.

Eighteen

The beer-bellied old drifter in the hot springs blurted something about Schubert and Hitler, something about getting his. He talked while I floated in the murky, algae-filled, rotten-eggs-smelling water about a poor, hang-gliding doctor who got stuck in the leeward wind rotor on a high ridge and smashed into the ground. Found him with his head cut off by a broken crossbar. All the sky apes, he said, hung out on the ground while someone stupid enough gave it a test shot—wind dummies. But never him. This guy's no dummie. Loud now, his short brown hair damp and slicked back, he's waving his hands and talking about hang-gliding all over the country and these hippy chicks he met at a Rainbow Gathering out in North Carolina. Ran around in the hills taking peyote and all these babes took their shirts off. Total gas.

"I even taught for a few years at this girls' school," he said, while a dark-skinned older man with stringy white hair eased into the tub, "up out of Bridgeport. What a great job. I coached girls' volleyball, I taught math . . . and then one fine day they rewrote my job description so I couldn't get it." He winked and licked his lips: "But I got them, in the eighth grade, the little sweethearts." He rubbed his silver chest hair and leaned way back to look at the evening sky. He closed his eyes and rolled his head around—I heard something pop in his neck. My sores and cuts burned in the sulfurous water; lithium and forgetfulness. Peace in the heat. Nick finally took his shorts off underwater and slipped them up onto the muddy bank.

After getting fired, turned out, the sky ape had decided not to be anyone's commodity anymore; decided other people were going to be his commodity. Invested in a chain of topless bars in the Southwest. "T&A," he announced, "I give them what they want. Now I just put the card in the cash machine."

His watch alarm went off in the grass.

He got up and wiped off, said something about a TV show and walked off across the meadow. Back at his big brown Chevy van he closed the door. A British couple who'd also been soaking offered Nick and me Budweiser long-necks. I popped one open, leaned back against the rock wall of the tub, and sucked up the foamy suds those beers always seem to have. The man, short and sallow with hollow cheeks, worked in an old mountaineering shop outside London. He said he loved reading about the epic, monstrous Himalayan climbs, knew all the names—Chris Bonnington, Dougal Haston, Joe Brown, Don Whillans, Boardman and Tasker—but didn't think himself up to alpine climbing, to the big mountains. He'd heard about Tuolumne in a British magazine, and he and his companion, Virginia, took up climbing just for "Tooloom" Meadows. Two weeks of delicate balance moves on California granite; the big, Wild West. Virginia took her eyes off Nick to watch her boyfriend talk while she dragged on a Marlboro. She was very tan and her face looked unnervingly strong.

The Englishman told heroic Himalayan tales of the way it ought to be: Don Whillans, the great English tongue, is on an international Everest expedition. Things are a mess at base camp. The Italians are pissed at the Germans, the Germans think the French are slowing things down. Foreign fluency suffers heavily under fatigue. Two Germans enter the British tent: "Vhillans, haf you heard about ze Vorld Cup Soccer Finals? Vee have beaten you at your national shport." Whillans: "Well, that's brilliant chaps. Of course, we've beaten you twice at yours now, haven't we?"

Lycra appalled the Englishman. While Nick looked at me a little askance, the Brit insisted UK climbers were rugged types, outdoorsy. Americans and their colorful ropes, bright outfits, sunglasses, tights—ruins the ambience.

"Must be wonderful," Nick mumbled without looking at the guy, "to live in a real frontier country like Britain. You know, rough and ready, and all."

Since they'd been in the States the Brits had been knocked out by the amount of choice. On the way down to the springs, Virginia had gone in to buy smokes: "A box of Marlboros, please."

"Lights, 100s, regulars . . . ?"

"What?"

"What kind of Marlboros?"

"Marlboros."

Down comes a carton. Good Lord, she can't believe the size of it. "No, God no. Just a box, please."

"That is a box."

"Isn't it ten boxes?"

"You mean a pack?"

"Yeah, I suppose so. Twenty smokes."

"Soft pack or hard?"

The man with white hair smiled softly to himself, then got out of the springs and walked barefoot back to his own van—a white Ford parked next to the sky ape's Chevy. A halfhour later the sun put on a shameless show, reds ripping out across the basin ranges, the northeast face of Mount Morrison to the west and of Ritter fifty miles north both pink, whole battlements of orange and rose. When we'd dried off in the breeze, we all walked back toward the cars. The grass was prickly under my feet, and there were spots of white mud. Back by the vehicles, the white-haired man sat outside his red Ford van in a lawn chair. A fluted glass half full of red wine rested on the salt flat at his feet. He played flamenco guitar in the sunset. When he'd finished and was taking a drink, Virginia asked if he'd know a request.

"Well," he said, "there are four thousand thirty-one flamenco songs and I know three."

"'Wandering Lambs'?"

He played, and the reds reached higher over the darkening mountains until only the summit of Mount Ritter

still burned. With stars appearing over the black eastern silhouette of the White Mountains, the old man thumped and
brushed his strings.

"Have you all seen what I do?" he asked, suddenly
stopping and standing up. He clambered awkwardly into
his van and slammed its sliding door. A few yards off, the
sky ape's television generator whirred; suburban blue light
flickered around the interior. TV gunshots and car tires
sounded shrill and tinny in the wind. Nick looked me fully
in the eyes, stunned. By all of it. I nodded back: "Yes! I
know! Madness!" His mouth opened and he laughed
silently in disbelief, as if he were thinking, "Yes! This is it!
This is it."

The old man slid back the door again. He put a piece of
varnished redwood burl at our feet and gave Nick a flashlight.

"Shine it on the stage there," he said, "I'm Uncle
Henry. This is Cousin Jack. He's what you call a limber-
jack."

A wooden cowboy hung from a string on the neck of
the guitar. Leather boots and gold spurs rested on the stage,
right in the spotlight. Out came a song about Cousin Jack
and Uncle Henry and their driving up and down and how
they'd been to parties, good times, helped out at bad times
but always stuck together and as the guitar shook, Cousin
Jack clicked his heels and did jig after jig on the redwood
burl on the salt flat. Nick stared at the ground; I thought he
was shaking a little when the music stopped.

"Any you ever seen a balloon dog? I do balloon sculpture too." Cousin Jack and the guitar disappeared. Henry

started blowing and twisting. Virginia smiled at the gift: a pink balloon poodle.

"And here's some passes to the harvest festival I'm on my way to up in Bend, Oregon. That's mostly what I do. Harvest festivals, craft fairs, earth festivals, Gatherings. If you ever see me at one, say hi. I also do private parties. Here's my card."

Nineteen

Black steel ski lifts rumbled up Mammoth Mountain in dry summer heat, hauling mountain bikes and riders high over dirt-brown, defoliated slopes. All over the ski runs neon eco-tourists bombed down the volcano, shredding soil, ripping it up with carbon-fiber frames and rock-shox. The Mammoth Inn Chateau, with its faux-Swiss gingerbread styling, seemed naked without snow on its eaves or skis against its outside walls. Three empty tour busses idled in front, their exhaust stinking up a clear mountain morning.

Kyla took off her batiked purple sweatshirt and squatted down by the new royal blue backpack she'd finally bought at the shop. On the parking lot asphalt she sorted our meals, the heaviest part of the load: breakfasts—bag of granola, dried peaches, dried apricots, oatmeal, herbal tea; lunches—trail mix, dried hummus, a dozen Powerbars, more dried fruit, six chocolate bars; dinners—pasta with dried pesto sauce, dried lentil soup, dried black beans. Seven silver bracelets rattled on her wrists as her filthy, elegant hands divided the food into three nylon stuff sacks.

The sleeping bag goes in the bottom of the pack because it's bulky but light. Then, along the middle, in close to your back, goes the food and other heavy stuff—I took the little gas stove, dented aluminum fuel bottles and blackened pots. Kyla took the blue nylon tent.

"Where's your friend, Nick?" she asked. "Didn't he want to come with us?"

He'd said something about seeing the Grateful Dead out in Nevada.

"They're so bad on tape," Kyla said, pushing a strand of hair behind her ear. "But I hear you have to be there." I'd gone to about twelve Dead shows in high school, but none since. Kyla wanted to know why I'd stopped, and I didn't have an answer.

Then, synthetic thermal underwear, wool socks, synthetic fleece sweaters, rain jacket and pants, wool hat and gloves, utensils, bug repellent, pocket knife, compass, topo map to the Minarets quadrangle (laminated with clear packing tape), sunglasses, sunscreen, toothbrush, waterproof matches, *Naturalist's Guide to the Sierra Nevada*, water filter, aluminum cups, biosuds, steel wool for cleaning pots, toilet paper and trowel for digging shit pits, sleeping pads, pot holder, first-aid kit. My climbed-out fingers ached as I packed, and an opened scab let blood run down the back of my hand. I stood up to stretch and looked around at all the cars.

"The gorge was rad," I said. "But I think I'm pretty into summits. Career substitutes." Kyla sat back on the ground and rubbed her eyes. I went on: "Massive achievements with zero significance. Pick a line and do it." Kyla stopped rubbing and squinted up at me. She reached out and put a hand on my ankle.

"Nick's not as weird as you are, is he?" She kneaded my calf muscle until it tickled.

"Can't you relate?" I asked. "At least I'm taking time out from life and still getting a daily goal fix."

She'd driven the Ghia up the night before, topless with the roof down in the dead valley heat, starving because she couldn't find anything edible between Santa Cruz and the Mammoth grocery store. Her senior thesis on passing was coming along—passing for white, black, gay, straight, male, female—and she'd mentioned maybe moving to Berkeley. Maybe try to work on the restaurant scene, make beautiful desserts, see how things went between us. She bent to the ground, slipped a strong, skinny arm through a shoulder strap, and heaved.

"I'm glad," she said, panting and scrunching her nose as she hoisted, "maybe it's sexist of me, but I'm glad . . . " Up on her knee the monstrous blue pack lurched suddenly to the right, out of control—she looked frightened; sweat beaded on her nose and her face flushed. Then, with a twist of her hips, she slipped it around onto her back and bent forward under the weight. Muscles stood out on her tan thighs as she hoisted the harness into place.

"I'm just psyched women don't get burdened with those kind of stupid hang-ups." She got the buckle snapped and tightened the belt. "You need to live for now, Dan. I'm serious. I think this is a good reason for you to spend more time with me." She smiled widely, then winced under the weight of her pack. I got my pack on too, and we looked at each other in disbelief.

"I totally forgot about this part," she said. "Oh my God."

"Me too." The load was murderous. I felt like an out-of-shape Atlas, like I could barely lift my feet.

Packs off, we dumped the whole mess back onto the pavement and started to rethink:

"How much granola do we really need?"

"How many Powerbars are we going to eat after all? Both a fork and a spoon?"

"Can't one cup be plate, bowl and cup?"

Packs trimmed to survivable size, we took a shuttle bus from parking lot to trailhead. Kyla told me how she'd first found backpacking on a high school trip—nobody in her family had ever done anything like it, and they were con-fused by her desire. Now she saw that trip as one of a series of small conversion experiences, one of her best-ever glimpses from the outside in at her suburban home with liv-ing room soda fountain and pinball machines.

I studied the map while we wound around on the little road—Red's Meadow, Devil's Post-pile, Mount Ritter, Mount Banner.

"Think we can make it to Minaret Lake tonight?" I asked. "I mean, if we haul and don't take too long of a lunch?" Kyla was looking off toward the Minarets and had her fingers out a window in the warm breeze. She'd changed earrings to a series of silver studs. She chuckled at my question, looked lovingly from me to the map and back again, then shook her head without answering.

"Well?" I asked.

"Does it matter?"

Had she misheard me? "Does what matter?"

"Where we get to tonight. Or ever."

"Oh, come on. Don't you want to make Garnet Lake tomorrow?"

She looked at me like there was something I was just too sweet and innocent to understand. She put her hand in mine and looked back out the window.

"You'll be all right," she said.

On the trail, we walked above the headwaters of the river called San Joaquin in a part of the mountains recently named the Ansel Adams Wilderness—out of the sagebrush scrub of the eastern slope of the Sierra and into alpine high country. Once we got over the initial misery of forty-pound loads and leather boots, once our skin and muscles decided to put up with it, Kyla was out of her mind with wildflowers, telling me about pollination in delphiniums, monkshood, crimson columbine, lupine; she picked leaves of miner's lettuce and chewed it while we slogged up a rip-rapped switchback. She wondered aloud if you could maybe go without bringing food up here—probably not, she decided, especially if you were vegetarian.

"Hey!" she yelled at me. "Hey, you! Look up."

I stopped. "At what?" Above were white fir and Jeffrey pines. I thought maybe she'd seen a great bird, or maybe a Stealth bomber from the secret air base they had out here somewhere.

"Just look up," she said, "all around you . . . " She was talking happily to the sky, not looking at me, turning around and around with her big brown boots in the dust. "Where

exactly do you think you're charging off to?" Now she had
her hands on her hips.

Frankly, I had no idea where I was charging to. It just
seemed like we ought to make time, not just loiter around
the wilderness. I dropped my pack and pulled out a Powerbar. A river splashed down a canyon to my left. Kyla walked
up and looked me in the eye, kissed me lightly with sweaty
lips, then marched on past. I took a deep breath, and
watched her go. After a while, when she hadn't looked back
once, I shouldered my pack and followed. She seemed absurdly small and burdened under her towering, overloaded
pack; all I could see from behind were her little legs poking
out from below.

A couple of miles later we stopped for lunch at a plush
green meadow with a pond nearby and a granite crag overhead shaped like a flattened ice-cream cone. Seemed early
to me to be stopping, but Kyla went ahead and cut pieces of
jalapeño jack cheese and homemade walnut-onion bread
she'd baked just for this first day. With filtered creek water
she mixed up a cup of hummus and laid out a picnic on a
boulder.

Fifteen miles a day was standard with the guys—up
before dawn and marching, brief skinny-dipping lunch
break, then plodding until dark. Nobody admitting the ag-
ony in their boots. Everyone walking a little too fast to be
comfortable. At every pause one of us would whip out the
map and compass:

"All right men, looks like we've gone about ten-and-a-
quarter miles and we're at about nine thousand five hundred feet elevation."

"How far to Black Rock Pass?" Squinting, sweating and bucking up.

"Few miles. If we haul we ought to be able to make Big Arroyo by dark. Make sixteen miles for the day. We'd have a shot at Rattlesnake Creek tomorrow." At camp we'd fall down against our packs, blistered feet throbbing, and pass out shortly after bolting down a vile freeze-dried mess.

After two hours of lying naked in the sun on a rock, Kyla had to be begged to move on. She definitely sympathized more with cats than dogs, more with lizards than mountain goats. A mile-and-a-half later she stopped walking, put down her pack, and said we were at a great camping spot.

"What?"

"Well it's really flat and grassy and close to the stream."

"But we've barely gone anywhere." I couldn't believe it.

Four o'clock and it was going to be light until eight. Just taking it easy. Maybe a little lesson to learn. I think every outdoorsy guy dreams about backpacking with a girl-friend sometime—something so primal about it, so Arca-dian. The old American wilderness honeymoon. But Kyla's spin on adventure was a revelation: enjoy.

She fell down on her knees and laughed hysterically as gender roles plagued us: I broke big sticks for a fire with a hunk of granite while she got water from the stream. I hung the extra food by a rope from a tree branch (out of reach of brown bears), while she set up the stove to make dinner. I set up the tent; she zipped the sleeping bags together—I built the house, she made the nest. After dinner, she de-

manded we sleep in the tent. The open air was nice, great to
see the stars, but kind of cold.

"You'll be all right outside," I insisted, nodding, "my
body's really warm."

She bit her lip and paused, then said, "Yeah right."
Barely concealing her amused contempt, she took both
sleeping bags into the tent.

"What on earth are you doing?" Kyla mumbled in her sleep.

"Six a.m. Dawn. Time to jam, build a fire and boil
water."

She smiled briefly and tried to hold onto me, to not let
me get up, then buried herself back inside the bags. At ten-
thirty, the sun well up over the tree tops, after I'd already
gone through all the t'ai chi I knew, all the stretching,
drooled over a rock wall up on Clyde Minaret and read the
chapter on glaciation again, Kyla crawled out of the tent in
her dark blue thermal underwear. She sat in the sun quietly
and warmed up, rubbed a hand against her tangle of matted
hair. She made nettle tea and told me to be quiet so she
could hear the birds.

Clyde Minaret—a monstrous, craggy tower in the distance. A famous climb; Dad had been talking about it
for years. Absolutely wild to rock-climb in the backcountry. Maybe I'd come up here again someday. Nick would
never go for it though, too psycho and self-abusive for him.
Those routes in the gorge had shown him the light—
painless glory.

"Will you do a sun salutation with me?" Kyla said.

"Just once and you never have to do it again? Come on, don't laugh, just do it with me." She stood up. "Take off your shoes so your feet are really on the ground. And stand over here next to me, in the sun. Raise your arms, then open them wide. It's supposed to be you're offering your face and chest to the morning." She exhaled. I exhaled too. "Now do another."

I almost lost my balance, and as I held my arms out, all the muscles I'd pulled climbing with Nick let me know they were still pulled. But it was a wonderful way to stand and breathe the cool delicious air, and when I closed my eyes, my eyelids burned red on the inside. Kyla. Then she jabbed her finger in my exposed ribs and I buckled over into the side of the tent.

At eleven o'clock that morning we stopped for lunch in a gulch with a roaring stream. We left the packs on the bank and took food out to a broad, flat boulder in the water. Just upstream a waterfall dropped through the air and foamed into a pool. Along the bank were violets and buttercups; young willows crowded up against firs. Trout rippled in holding patterns, facing upstream. Kyla waded back to the bank and cleared all the rocks and twigs out of a small patch of grass, then spread our shirts and shorts in a broad sheet. We lay together and made love, clean from the creek, warm and dry from the sun, and took turns looking down into the soil and up at the trees; all that furless skin on a warm summer day with swallows dogfighting and squirrels working for a living.

Life simplified the way it always does backpacking—eating, sleeping, shitting, walking, eating, sleeping, shitting. But hiking over gentle passes on wide, firm trails in good weather without mosquitos, never walking far enough to get sore or even sick of it, bathing and making love outdoors, getting plenty of sleep and eating well, the backcountry felt like an enormous Edenic park. If wilderness is anywhere something could eat you, then I'd been putting in the predator myself: gravity.

Twenty

The fast-paced world of shoe repair. Time to talk toluol-based adhesives and rubber gradients. Cobbler's knives and power sanders. Maybe two thousand dollars for a pneumatic press. I told the shop manager we had a major cash leakage—four or five customers a week needed their rock climbing shoes resoled, and we just mailed the shoes off. It'd be beautiful for Nick and me, our own little program. No more folding T-shirts, totally flexible hours. A real craft, fixing real things with my hands, learning a trade and, best of all, working with bad-ass power tools. The manager loved the idea of keeping the work right here. He put up the money and told me to start practicing on our rentals.

No problem. I grabbed a trashed old pair of green Verticals ready to breathe new life into them. I propped a heat gun up against a glued-on sole, let it warm, then gave it a pull. No luck. Nick suggested we get serious, head into the back. Down in the ski shop, Teenage Fan Club on the tape deck, French posters of women climbing naked, I pulled harder, this time with pliers. No luck, although one of the stitched seams on the upper appeared to be parting a little.

Nick muscled me aside, got his body under it and yarded. Still no luck, though a couple more stitches parted.

"Back to the heat gun," I said.

"Really got to break down that goddam glue," Nick added. I propped the gun back up there and we walked up front for a cup of coffee.

The homeless man named Trip stood by the cash register, shivering and talking to our ace salesman, the six-foot-two ponytailed backcountry ski guru. Trip had short dreadlocks, a braided cord around his neck, and his chest muscles stood out like the proverbial flagstones above abdominal cobblestones—the guy was ripped. He came in daily asking to wash car windows. This time he looked terrible, an overcoat pulled tight, thinned out a little, paling.

"I was . . . am . . . wondering," he said to the guru, "if you had any, like, work I could do or anything."

The guru said he'd look. He walked off into the back, dragging his feet to keep his too-loose Birkenstocks from flipping off with each step. Asked everyone. The new assistant manager, who'd been changing things, showing sympathy, wasn't around to come up with something real. The guru came back fingering the tail of his hippy-cloth belt and looked around to make sure nobody was watching. Trip was shivering, but trying not to show it. The guru reached into the register and took out a five-dollar bill; he took the heat for a bad cash total when the time came.

The New American Male: the guru's girlfriend had gotten a job on the Pacific Stock Exchange, was making a fortune, had bought them a modest home. He just worked at the shop to pay bills, talked about maybe someday teaching high school, spent the vast majority of his time backcountry skiing, climbing and looking great. In the war of the sexes, he'd won.

"What you guys working on?" he asked.

I'd forgotten. Heat! I could suddenly smell burning rubber. I spilled coffee on the Swiss Army Knife display and sprinted into the back. Bubbles were just rising in the sole rubber when I flicked off the gun. Old, embedded sweat oozed out of every filthy pore of the leather as I wrestled it onto the iron jack. With pliers locked on I got my shoulder into it and pulled. Nick tapped me frantically on the shoulder as I increased leverage, but I ignored him.

"Do you mean to do that?" asked the manager. He stood suddenly behind me in a pressed shop T-shirt. Nick had vanished.

The entire sole ripped away at once and shredded leather from the midsole dangled off its underside. The manager looked personally wounded as he stood over the disemboweled remains of the shoe, then made a note on his clipboard and walked off. The guru passed by and he too took a close look at the carnage.

"Go for it," he said, and winked. He walked on out to the back lot looking for an old man named Clayton who lived there. Clay grew tomatoes in the dirt between buildings, perpetually wore a blue fishing hat and oil-stained blue windbreaker, and was usually too drunk to walk. While I tried to heat up another shoe, I watched the guru lean against the huge old false-woody station wagon in which Clay and his son drank bourbon. The guru's neurotic Labrador had been getting sick on the little piles of chicken bones Clay threw out the window.

Then, the glue: the source revealed of childhood tantrums over airplane models. Twenty minutes into smearing this noxious, clear goop onto the shredded remains of a hundred-and-fifty-dollar pair of shoes, goop determined by the state of California to cause brain, central nervous system and respiratory damage as well as profound mood swings and anxiety, and I noticed that I'd completely stopped thinking—nothing but a dull cerebral throb. Glue had somehow dripped onto my sandals and now even down into my wool socks. My eyes and nose were running. With the shoe only half covered, I put down the glue brush and stumbled out blinking to sit on the back stoop. As my brain defogged I thought about Kyla. On the phone that morning she'd asked if I was still willing to take her climbing.

Clay had finished his bourbon and was throwing the cardboard from our loading dock into a pile by his car. He'd take it down to the recycling yard for redemption value. Redemption. And I was trying to save soles. Clay looked around in a pile of garbage and I was peeling dried glue off my hands when I heard a crash. He lay face down on a pile of cardboard boxes. When I got closer, he turned his head, mumbled something, agreed to a hand up.

"Hanging out in this lot fifteen years," he said. "Day like this I should be out fishing on the lake."

Around here? What lake?

He took out a small pair of pliers and stooped over to our handleless faucet. He stood with the hose for a long time watering down his pile of cardboard, getting it good and soaked before selling it by the pound. Must have known somebody down at the recycling yard who'd let the high weight slide. Clay Jr. shuffled over to help—his back was so stiff he could barely walk. Half his ass hung out of his pants and he seemed sheepish around his father, a commanding presence.

Twenty-one

Kyla came down from campus one warm day on her mountain bike with fresh-picked sage wrapped around the handlebars and orange poppies and white jasmine woven into her hair. In her fanny-pack she had two big echinacea flowers, prickly purple spheres that made our mouths tingle and water. We rode dirt trails together high in the hills over Monterey Bay, and at a eucalyptus grove with a view out to sea Kyla opened her pack again—she'd picked ten big, ripe guavas at the campus organic farm.

She told me she'd just applied to a graduate program at a similar farm down in Big Sur—biodynamic horticulture and alternative medicine. She'd live in a tent, on the ground, growing the food she ate and cooking it with a community. She wanted to get into the healing arts and she'd heard this place wasn't too New Agey. She said that stuff had been bugging her lately—all the wide-eyed good vibes. The farm's fields, she told me, were on fertile hillsides in what had been a near-utopic land of native peoples—mild climate, plenty of fish and fruit, apparently very little intertribal war. The millennia-old cultures had been quickly obliterated by slave-driving Spanish missionaries, but down on the farm a sense of place was once again being cultivated.

"What about moving back to Berkeley?" I asked.

"Oh, I don't know," she responded, "maybe till I find out if I got in."

We walked our bikes away from the trail to a small field surrounded by oaks. Kyla put down her bike, took off her tank top and hung it on the handlebars. She took off her shorts and sat down naked on them with the guavas in her hands. I too stripped and sat down. Bare skin can be startling in daylight—pale, hairy and sweaty—but also just bare. I couldn't quite accept nakedness as more natural than clothing—it seemed about as natural as a human without tools. She was preoccupied with the fruit as she pried a guava open with her thumbs and licked out its jelly, then pried open another for me. As she handed over the torn, slimy green half to me she pointed out how wonderfully vulvic it was. I licked out its jelly and on the hard ground she moved over on top of me, still holding her fruit. There was something disturbingly distant in her face as we made love almost without moving; her mood shifted not at all from the content calm of the bike ride. Conversation continued, and so did the guavas.

"Hello," she said, in a normal tone, looking down at my forehead. She smiled, as always, with just the corners of her mouth, and bit mock-ferociously into another fruit.

"Hello."

"Don't move," she said.

We both got goosebumps from a sea breeze and a mosquito landed on my shoulder. She slapped it, flicked it off, then smeared guava junk on my lips.

"I don't know why I like sex so much more outside," she said, when we were sitting again. "Maybe it's because all my bad experiences were indoors. I kind of dread beds. Too many guys who freaked out that I didn't like buck and scream and fake orgasms and then they'd project their inadequacy all over me. Calling me frigid." She licked half of yet another guava. "I even went on the pill for a while, which I will never do again for anybody."

She saw a plant with long, shiny, dark green leaves. She walked over to it, and I noticed a mountain biker in a Team Angst jersey passing on the nearby road. He looked up, then quickly looked away.

"It's yerba santa," Kyla said. "It's Indian chewing gum. Put it on your tongue. I can totally keep mine there all day, like a little natural flavor-pack." For a while it was sweet and complex, but then I made the mistake of chewing it and it became horribly bitter. She laughed when I spit it out. She kept hers for a long time, swore it was her favorite taste. A fog bank was visible along the western horizon, lingering offshore, probably engulfing San Francisco seventy miles north.

We rode fast through the forest and around steep turns until the fire road fed out onto Highway 1. On the cliff by the Brussels sprout fields Kyla said again that it surprised her to find herself with a man; she'd been having fun with me, but was still curious about women. Penetration, aggression, performance anxiety and ego-involvement with sex had all left her cold; her skin had suffered and she'd been in therapy for her periods of deep depression.

I told her about my string of college bulimic manic-depressive girlfriends, including the last one who'd dumped me. I mentioned how I'd started wondering how many women were like that—maybe because of the impossible demands on them—how the symptoms had been shared by everyone from the Type-A dumper to one who read nothing but children's picture books and another who was off on a Navajo reservation teaching English. We kicked a footbag on an empty beach for hours and scrambled along cliffs above the waves. A cave exposed by low tide, Kyla said, led two miles back up into the forest behind campus. We rode home to the house well after dark in a cold northwesterly breeze. We locked our bikes on the redwood deck, and when we walked through the front door I heard a whisper.

"A man!"

The whole living room was filled with young women sitting on the floor. Carmen's discussion section on eating disorders was having a potluck. They dropped their forks and conversation stopped while I fled into Kyla's room. As I fell asleep trying to imagine what they'd all brought to eat, I could hear Carmen leading them through an exercise—they took turns telling the group they were coming out of the closet, even if they weren't, just to understand the feeling.

Twenty-two

I lay on the pine needles for a moment after waking up and tried to pick out morning constellations between the treetops. Then I got up and stuffed my sleeping bag. The smell of campfires and food had blown out of Camp 4 and cold high-country air had come down into the valley. I whispered to Nick that it was time. He moved a little inside his old down bag. The rack of pro clanked on the tailgate when I pulled it out of its crate, waking a Saint Bernard under a truck. In the east the night sky reddened behind the black mass of Half Dome. Nick appeared from the darkness with his pack, carrying his latest pair of Spanish climbing shoes, stunned at being awake. We'd been doing too much of a hundred feet here, a few hundred there; most of the time we didn't even get to the top of anything. I wanted to bag a major feature, a peak, something with a summit.

We parked near the base of El Capitan. Steam drifted up in peaks and valleys from the Merced River as a wisp of a woman in a chartreuse windbreaker made pancakes on a Coleman stove. Her family stood around shivering and drinking coffee. High up on the prow of El Capitan the

Wall of the Early Morning Light glowed with the dawn.
Dad had told me that the East Buttress, the far right-hand
edge of the Captain, wouldn't be way out of our league. He
thought we should try some more short routes first, get
some more experience. But he admitted that if we wanted
to do big walls some day, this was a crucial step. He just
thought it might be a little premature.

The meadow spread out below the wall like a cathedral
floor; an enormous oak had dropped a few huge limbs and
stood out like a lone baobab. The trail led through sparse
gallery forest straight to the Nose—the main buttress of the
biggest part of the wall. The classic Yosemite big wall. One
of the most famous rock-climbs in the world—thirty-two
pitches, at least three days for a standard team. The Nose's
features became distinct as we approached: the Sickle
Ledge down low; the long, clean Stoveleg Cracks leading to
Dolt Tower, an early bivouac; El Cap Towers; Texas Flake;
Boot Flake; the Great Roof, marking the transition from
the lower apron of the wall to the magnificent upper dihedral. It had become almost a commonplace that if climbing
were a religion, the upper dihedral of the Nose was a fitting
cathedral. Cold as my hands were, they sweated in the
pockets of my climbing pants.

Dad had no plans to do the Nose. I was nowhere near
ready for it, perhaps years away. I'd have to be able to move
quickly up hard cracks and run rope systems like second
nature; I'd need the absolute mental strength not to feel
lost in the Captain's vast spaces—a sort of private, recrea-
tional Valley of Death. Some guys seemed to have that pres-

ence of mind naturally; I did not. The Nose would have to come in the right order for me, after Washington Column—the classic starter wall—after Half Dome.

Stupendously high and utterly quiet; without sun making it shine, the wall kept to itself. No horrendous approach, no vast talus field: just flat meadow, a short rise, and then three thousand vertical feet of quiet white stone. There was no breeze. At the base we passed empty ravioli cans and shreds of toilet paper. I found a small chunk of aluminum swaged onto a cabled wire loop called a "bashie." I'd heard that on technical aid routes (as opposed to free climbing, in which the gear is used only as a safety net, while the climbing is done with hands and feet) guys would place the aluminum blob in a small pocket or groove and smash it into conforming with the pocket by hitting it with a hammer. Standing up very gently on a loop of cord attached to the bashie, they'd gain a few feet, moving gently so as not to pop anything out. For hundreds of feet at a time they'd inch up on marginal placements, none of which could take the impact of a fall—if one popped under the climber's weight, they all would. And he would fly. Lying on a slab at the base, the little piece of metal had fallen a long way. I put it in my pocket.

Only two hundred feet off the ground, under an enormous roof of smooth pinkish stone, a guy with scraggly brown hair was just waking up in his PortaLedge—like a window washer bivied at the twentieth floor mezzanine of a three-hundred-floor building. The framed hammock hung entirely free of the overhanging wall. Closer in, against the rock, his partner still slept. Two white haul bags hung beside them, moving slightly like sides of beef in a meat cooler's fan. A calm and oceanic experience.

The man rubbed his eyes and looked over at the Cathedral Spires. Out of a haul bag he pulled a carton of orange juice. A few hundred feet above him were two more PortaLedges, still motionless. A thousand feet farther were two more. The route was Mescalito; a guy I knew had spent seven days on it. They'd stopped talking much after the second. He once told me big wall climbing was more work than he'd ever done on a construction site; that endless pulling up of ropes, jumaring, hauling loads; the climbing itself and the hours upon hours of waiting in the sun belaying.

We moved up through oaks to the first talus field. We had come to the far end of the low overhangs below the black dioritic inclusion known as North America Wall. It must have spanned 75,000 square feet of rock and did have the shape of the continent, with Baja California wandering out into the Pacific and Central America and the Gulf of Mexico perfectly in place. The Great Lakes and Alaska didn't require any real leap to see. We passed the starts of South Seas and Pacific Ocean Wall, then North America Wall itself: weeks of no sound but wind and the tapping of metal on stone; a broad but unchanging view; exposure, tedium, fatigue, tension and total peace. Voluntary journeys scribed onto a geolith.

More garbage. We were on open talus now, hopping from boulder to boulder, approaching another group of trees. The wall shot straight into the ground—no transition, no place where wall gave way to earth. Just an over-hanging massivity. We passed under New Jersey Turnpike and Atlantic Ocean Wall. Then Iron Hawk, named, like Wings of Steel, for the means of flight; then Aurora, Tangerine Trip, Lost in America, Zenyatta Mondatta, Zodiac, Lunar Eclipse, Born under a Bad Sign. The guy who'd done Mescalito said you got so tired on big walls you couldn't think about ecology if you wanted to: you just sat on your ledge like a chain-gang worker with the flu and moaned. Garbage dropped out of your hands. Paper bags full of human shit burst on the ground.

Although the morning sun lit the upper rim of the wall, and the tips of Half Dome and Sentinel Rock to the east were beginning to glow, the enormous volume of space beneath the southeast face of El Capitan lay in shade. The bright publicity of daylight and the sounds of tour buses and cars were absent.

My peripheral vision took in only the lowest portion of El Capitan: the rest of the wall reached indeterminately above. So total was its presence, so still the air and so quiet the morning, I might have been in the deepest of canyons or most remote of mountain sanctuaries. I looked out across acres of broken rock—fallen over time—and up to the East Buttress itself; where the massif ended it formed a twelve-hundred-foot prow of stone whiter than the bulk of El Cap. It could well turn out to be too long for us. Not a notoriously hard climb, but long and classic, a grade up for us. Nick stopped walking and looked along the buttress's corners and cracks. He got out his camera and lingered at what he'd really rather be doing.

Right before me I heard splashing and spattering, but could see nothing wet. The sound was constant and steady, like the trickle of a grotto, but there was no stream, no waterfall. I looked up along the mass of El Cap for wet streaks, along the base for a spring—nothing, but still the sound of a light rain. Before me in a twenty-foot circle were wet rocks and little splashes spraying about them, throwing drops into the cracks. I stopped on a square-cut block the size of a small car, and looked up. Fifty feet out from the wall a perfect column of drops rained straight down out of blue sky.

Nick stood directly opposite me in his black pants, white T-shirt and cap, on the other side of the column; we both walked slowly around it with eyes on the sky. I thought of Lafayette Bunnell, the U.S. Cavalry doctor who was on the first expedition of white Americans to see Yosemite. Upon entering the valley in 1851 with the Mariposa Battalion—tracking down the Yosemite Indians—Bunnell fell suddenly behind the regiment when he saw El Capitan. A rearguard major called out to him:

"You had better wake up from that dream up there," he said, "or you may lose your hair . . . some of the murdering devils may be lurking along this trail to pick off stragglers."

"If my hair is now required," the doctor responded, "I can depart in peace, for I have here seen the power and glory of a Supreme being; the majesty of His handy-work is in that 'Testimony of the Rocks.'"

There are times when, finally, the only adequate response to beauty is to walk away. We continued along the wall while a warm breeze stirred in the shade. We passed the magnificent roof that began Zodiac; hundreds of streaks of pastel pinks and tans shooting over a vast arch. On an overhanging aid wall like Zodiac, one would be in silent, immutable verticality for days on end—living for a moment in one's life with order and purpose.

More streaks and columns of pastels—some marble greens now among the pinks and grays; the rock appeared near-perfect, almost soft, not at all jagged or broken. We passed fixed lines coming down from Born under a Bad Sign—a notoriously terrifying and tenuous multi-day climb; the climbers had cached supplies at the base. All of it—the ropes, packs, bags—sat out on the exposed rock as if in the unchanging air of a desert. Nick stopped and stared. His overloaded little pack pulled his slender shoulders back and his neck stuck forward as he gazed. I imagined he was thinking about the wall, about the kinds of people who could do such things. Probably deciding that he was not such a person himself.

I sat down on a boulder to rest and thought how thirty years ago El Capitan was a barely charted Louisiana Purchase; now it was impregnated with stories and route names: The Shield, Genesis, the Muir Wall, the Heart Route, Jolly Roger, and Magic Mushroom—the latter climb put up by two teenagers from Canada who ate hallucinogenic mushrooms en route. A climber of the sixties may have had the fear and pleasure of the unknown, but now the psychic universe of the wall was overwhelmingly rich.

Twenty-three

Manzanita picked at our skin as we racked up in the dust at the base of the East Buttress. I started scrambling inside a deep, wide gash in the wall, and with my body splayed out across a chasm, I built an anchor a hundred feet up. Nick started the next pitch by trying a delicate move in a corner and almost immediately began to shake. He fell hard onto the rope and jerked me around until we were staring at each other point-blank. Infuriated and embarrassed, he thrashed back into position, and soon he was out of sight. Looking out of the chimney I had a narrow column of sky—a dead straight view unlimited above—confined on either side. Sun had spread well into the valley, and three RVs were parked by the Merced River below. I soaked in the peace and tried to stay warm.

No idea what was taking so long, I asked.

"Dan! You wouldn't believe this!"

"What? Aren't you at the belay?"

"Yeah, but there's ants everywhere!"

"Well don't kill any or they'll start biting!" It was true— the notorious Yosemite "grease ants," which, when crushed, emit an odor like rancid raisin juice that drives their entire tribe into a mad biting assault on human flesh.

"I'm trying not to but . . . "

"Isn't there a tree?"

"Yeah, but it's covered with ants!"

"Well, can't you sling it?"

"NO!"

I couldn't believe it. We had to make time. "Well, you've got tons of rope, just keep going and set the belay higher up!"

"How will I know where?"

"Just wherever you can get gear in!"

"But it's all covered with ants!! No, I'm coming back down!"

"What? What do you mean you're coming back down?"

Two women wearing helmets had appeared below and started uncoiling their ropes. After two hours we'd gone two hundred feet and had a long way to go. I shrieked at Nick to build a belay somewhere. Now. I was coming up.

"I'm just going to downclimb!" he yelled.

Unbelievable. Unspeakable. "What? And bail on the whole route?"

"I don't know!"

"Or just so I can deal with the ants?!!" No reply. No rope movement. These were not good signs in a climbing partner. I had a long, cold wait, shivering, trying to resist peeing in the chimney (in deference to anyone who might follow) and frantically adjusting my harness to relieve my collapsing testicles. It was a nasty little slot to hang in—oppressive and cold. With a trace of sensitivity, I made another query. He mumbled that he'd built an anchor and was off belay.

At last I could unclip. After a hundred feet of scrambling and stemming, I passed the tree in question. A few ants sauntered around one of its limbs; no hordes, no black swarming earth, no point in saying anything. Nick swore the tree had been black with ants thirty minutes before, engulfed by them. No idea where they'd gone. Swore to it. Then stopped talking. He didn't want to lead anymore: "Kind of shaken up, just not sure where to put in gear, feeling pretty far off the ground."

On a rust-colored, knife-blade arête we found outrageously fun climbing—holding this twelve-inch-wide rib of rock out in space, pulling up on big, secure holds. The angle eased and we moved quickly up terraces of granite hundreds of feet wide, up through patches of grass and across rolling, marbled slabs. At just about the route's halfway we had Powerbars and water on a stunning ledge—with our hands gripping the easternmost edge of the entire Captain, we could see clear to the ocean of white stone called Cloud's Rest.

"Uh oh. Dude," Nick mumbled, "clouds overhead. Danger. Danger." He wasn't much into the view. His face actually looked sick and he kept glancing around, everywhere but at me.

Huge thunderheads started to pour east, shadowed and brilliant. Directly above, a towering, gilded stormcloud spread and expanded. Nick shivered and said, "That monster black cloud could shaft us. And us without our rain jackets, once again. This could be our lethal lesson. I'm serious. We're in way over our heads, homer. I mean, we are way off the ground with a long, long way to go."

A ribbon of tiny golden spheres swirled into view, each shining ball hovering before my eyes as if to show off its symmetry and light. Like a swarm of angels, they whipped horizontally in front of us, rising and falling in a band with the wind. For a moment they blew straight up, sparkling quietly, then were all around us, then above, then spattering in a hundred drops of water down against the rock before soaring out from the wall. The waterfall I'd seen on the approach had found us again; afternoon winds blew it out into the sun like a kite string in a breeze. The drops evaporated on contact with the hot stone.

"Even this waterfall," Nick grumbled, rubbing his hands together, "this is kind of freaking me out. Those upper pitches could be totally unclimbable."

"You really want to bail?" I think I sounded pretty disgusted, and he was too vulnerable to call me on it. He couldn't meet my eyes and kept looking at the ground. I could almost watch him turn inward away from the route and the moment, wrongly suspecting that I was seething with contempt; his self-hatred did the rest of the job and without permission I racked up and led off. It took him a long time to follow and once he did he climbed nervously, muttering to himself and constantly chalking his hands. I was pretty scared about the storm too, but I wanted the top.

The weather moved fast, and the high-country darkened. Big streaks of rain hung out of the clouds like tendrils from a jellyfish. We started catching trans-Sierran winds out of the west as we climbed out to the upper slabs of the buttress. Then, after hours of uncertainty over the storm, after hundreds of feet of magnificent climbing, I emerged on top—a blissful rush of sweaty, sunburned, bleeding relief. Just as Nick arrived, the sun slipped below the horizon to the west, while to the east Half Dome stood in stunning relief—a ring of dark clouds underlined with gold descended around the dome like a halo of fleece. We packed up quickly, coiled the ropes, and jogged off to the big tree where the rappels began. As we slid down our ropes the hues of cloud and stone on Half Dome continued to shift, light and vapor painting and repainting the wall.

Back on the warm, even pavement of the road, Nick shook his head.

"Just thought we were screwed," he said. I think he glanced over to see if I'd forgiven him for cracking. He kicked a pebble along the road and said he thought he preferred the Owens River Gorge, didn't think he'd ever go in for big walls. In the darkness we could barely make out the top of the East Buttress, and I started wondering when old Aaron would be back. When we reached the car, the jet black of the Nose swooned against the stars. A few lights winked on up high, perhaps on Mescalito, maybe one on the Shield. We drove back to buy a hot shower with bluegrass on the car radio. In the trees known as the Jungle, on the Valley Rim above the Royal Arches route, a bonfire

burned—climbers sleeping out inadvertently. In the morning I ate early and walked out in the meadow to watch the
dawn. Then, back to town. Back to Kyla.

Twenty-four

Fresh focaccia and decaf Sumatra, Kyla stood on Walnut Street in Berkeley and tightened the straps on her leather sandals. Then she took a footbag out of her pocket and began kicking it around by herself. I held bites of dark chocolate truffle in my mouth, sipped coffee over them, and watched her. School over, she had her apartment back in Berkeley, was looking for direction. Waiting to hear about the farm.

Move in? With her? I mean . . . live together?

"You sleep there every night anyway," she said. Needling, having fun, and it was true. "Just this way I pay all the rent."

But move in? "I leave nothing there. No clothes. I never hang out there when you're not around. And it's your space—your dried flowers, your herbs, your cactus, even your bromeliad. Would we . . . would we mingle records?"

She held her cup of green tea high with one hand while she kicked the leather bag with the insides of her feet. Remaining centered. In one ear she had a green-and-blue macrame earth, in the other a white moon; they swung around while she played. A psychologist friend of my mother's waved from across the street—doing the North Berkeley circuit: Asiago bread from the Cheese Board, sushi from the Fish Market, across the street to Cocolat for a chocolate truffle; then the darkest of coffee from Peet's and a bench in the sunshine outside the Friends Meeting House. Kyla read to me from a book that Carmen had sent her called *The Grub Bag*, by Ida Jones.

"'We are all lost people in this world, do we need introduction? You've seen my curly head and glowing eyes a thousand times. And I know you when I see you, in the subway, on the street, our eyes caress each other's faces. Wanting to make love we've simply smiled and nodded recognition.

"'I touch your shoulder now, your breasts, your balls, and whisper the most secret of my thoughts.'" She stopped and looked at the cover. "What a trippy book."

A lanky, ruddy-skinned and evasive guy named Steve, an old friend, walked by with a baby. We'd dismembered G.I. Joes together for an entire summer once in his backyard. Each time they got shot, we made it permanent— heating pieces of wire to melt grotesque scars into their faces. When we began to grow out of the dolls, we cut off their heads and fired them across my backyard with their own cannon.

"Ouch," Kyla said. She clutched her belly. "Full baby need."

"No way."

"Who said anything about you?"

"Nobody. But . . . "

"I don't need a husband. I know a lesbian who totally had a gay guy get her pregnant."

A meat truck backfired and obscured my question: "Why gay?"

"My mom would probably even help out. She'd be psyched."

This was terrifying, not least because she could probably afford it. "No male in the picture at all, huh? Don't you think a father's kind of key?"

"Marriage is more dangerous than babies."

"But when did this come up?" She'd never so much as mentioned kids before. And what about having a job first? Or at least a clue about what kind of job you wanted? Could you just go ahead and have a baby because it sounded neat? Steve had apparently learned how to hold one; he also looked like he'd been trying to grow a mustache. A long-haired writer I knew strolled by in his trademark white T-shirt.

"Check this out," Kyla said, going back to the book as if it contained instructions I should heed, "'The revolution will kill us if we don't widen our vision.'" She'd been poring over cookbooks lately—*Moosewood*, *The Enchanted Broccoli Forest*, *The Tassajara Bread Book*—looking for cures, thinking about her someday vegetarian restaurant. "'Someone to eat with and some green among your spices,'" she read, "'are among the most important things to have in your kitchen, which can become a room into which you come smiling.' Maybe I should stick to cooking at home, I'd love to just never work."

I'd heard her say this before, and couldn't believe it. It seemed so unfeminist, or maybe postfeminist, or neo-feminist.

"What would you do?" I asked.

"Nothing. And bake bread. Does everybody have to do something all the time?"

"You don't mean that." Whenever she got onto this subject I wondered how her implied lover was supposed to be simultaneously anticareerist and a great provider.

"My mom got to do it," she said, then read on: "'Jars stacked on shelves revealing the different colors inside them, cacti on the windowsill . . .'"

But her dad was still a stranger to her. "Does marriage really spook you?" I asked, realizing all at once how great it sounded to me.

"Come on, I want to read. I just don't believe people should be artificially bonded to each other. You get bored." She turned back to the book: "'lilacs on the table, pictures on the walls, plenty of nails to hang things on . . .'"

"Monogamy?" I demanded, trying to feel out the dimensions of this gulf.

"What about you?" She put down the book and leaned forward to knead a thigh muscle.

"Absolutely."

"You really want arbitrary limits?"

"Yep. Big limits." I was getting very nervous very quickly.

"Well, there's something wrong with that. Anyway, listen: '. . . an ashtray, a reefer, a cat, and the eggs and tomatoes in that glass bowl will radiate with the desire to be joined and eaten.' This is why I'm so crazy about my bowls."

"Ok, I get it. Baby, but no commitment."

"Well, how about you? Commitment but no baby? Is that any less screwy?" Somehow I knew it was, but the question caught me off guard. Before I could think it through, Steve came back with a cup of coffee. He said he'd been doing some carpentry contracting, finally got himself a truck. Not much free time though. Kid's keeping him up all night.

"'But this isn't only a cookbook,'" Kyla read, "'and I sit here in my overstuffed chair imagining that maybe you and I could talk in a light, tilting dream, under the shade of an old rustling tree, about just things.'"

Afraid I wasn't listening, Kyla closed the book and went back to her green tea. After a brief chat, Steve walked off toward the bookstore on the corner and I looked at this woman Kyla, legs spread in the splits on a bench. Maybe I could be persuaded . . . I mean, I did want kids someday.

I sat on the bench beside her and picked up the *The Grub Bag*. In the uncomfortable quiet, Kyla humming some nameless tune with her mouth full of hot tea, I read a chapter to myself:

"1. Rice and Pilaf. I think that as the country falls into repression, the radicals hit the barricades, and the heads head for the mountains, eating will become the first thing on people's minds. . . . We who do the fighting can't expect it to be over in a month. Thinking concretely, one can see that to win, our healthy minds will need healthy bodies."

Twenty-five

The redheaded painter had painted herself and an old, pallid lover at an ornate oak table. They wore green jester's costumes and shared a meal: she cut into a single, oversized white pear, which oozed bright blood across the table; he carved greedily into a painting of the two of them in bed; on a serving tray a human heart was in flames. The room yawned cavernously behind them, with a checker-tiled floor and stone-arched windows in the background. Ottomans and overstuffed chairs littered the middle distance. Brynn had just bought the piece, and was ecstatic.

"It was either that or a car," she said, and poured me a tumbler of Petite Sirah.

Focused on an esthetically flawless future, Brynn had bobbed blond hair and wore a black beaded choker. She and her fiancé, Tracy, were high school friends of mine. Tracy had made the table around which we sat—he bought a slab of granite and welded together a burnished steel frame to support it. One corner of the slab was broken off and replaced with steel along a flush jagged line. The heavy oak chairs were late Arts and Crafts and on the wall hung two lead slabs with sheaths holding scrimshaw mummies.

134 D A N I E L   D U A N E

Natalie, a blue-eyed friend of theirs from Manhattan, had been working at Planned Parenthood. She was a year out of Wesleyan College and had been volunteering, making a difference. They'd just agreed to give her a salary and a title—family planning consultant.

"Who worries about that stuff, though," Natalie said, when I said I'd been reading some nature writers, some John Muir, Ed Abbey, Wendell Berry. "I mean, unless they have nothing else to worry about?"

Always alert, Brynn saw disaster coming—she didn't share my prejudices but respected and avoided them; since high school she'd seen me get defensive on too many embarrassing issues. She graciously showed us an intaglio of an emaciated man curled up in the corner of an empty black space. It hung over their iron bed on a wall of rust-washed plaster and reminded me of something Kyla'd said that morning as I left for the mountain shop—she'd been picturing herself dead recently, and didn't know why. Usually a passive death—hit by a car, drowning in a bathtub—but never entirely accidental. The fog that had bothered her when she was younger had returned and her therapist had suggested Prozac. Brynn offered Natalie more wine. I noticed Tracy had decorated the trim of their armoire with gold metallic paint.

"Like why aren't you reading Annie Dillard," Natalie said, "or Willa Cather? Women have a totally different take on nature and the earth, I think, so much less violating. So of course women's views have to be hushed up because they're so threatening."

Could the men really all be so privileged? Such an unlikely assortment of writers? It seemed possible, and I started running through my mental Rolodex, skipping quickly past Ed Abbey's notorious misogyny and remembering Drew's piece in the campus journal on ecofeminism and the politics of totality. I paused on John Wesley Powell, a Civil War veteran missing an arm, and started to mention Clarence King, but remembered he'd gone to Yale. Maybe she was right.

"Muir, though," I remembered at last, "the famous naturalist of Yosemite." Tracy looked a little bored and stared into his wineglass. I couldn't blame him for being distracted—his HIV positive father had just started getting AIDS-related illnesses. He shifted his feet on the architectural pine coffee table—it had the lines of a suspension bridge—and sank deeper into the fluffy, charcoal gray couch. An immaculate, athletic Francophile, he'd tried climbing a few times with me. He was an absolute natural and liked it all right; he just didn't care enough for all this fuss.

"John Muir?" Natalie said. "Are you kidding? The man-in-the-mountains guy? All those pictures of him surrounded by women in fancy clothes in San Francisco?"

But Muir came from dirt poor immigrant farmer stock and ran away from home!

"Yeah," she insisted, flipping back her hair, "but when I was staying at the Ahwahnee with my mom I saw some old pictures of him with Emerson and Teddy Roosevelt like a classic good old boy."

Dead, white and male, Muir certainly was, and the iconoclast always holds the trump card. Tracy brought up a water polo match we'd played together in high school and conversation swept on by.

I fingered my wineglass and watched the legs run down its sides. I'd been reading Muir's *My First Summer in the Sierra* and frankly could barely stand it. The elegy! Not Christianity, but "Mountianity." He had the same affliction that made Emerson "fear to think how glad I am." But he also lived an awfully strange life. His childhood on his Scottish father's farm in Wisconsin was virtually a term of enslavement, and his naturalism was partly a way of staying sane—out in the fields alone, plowing for thirteen-hour days as a little boy, he had to find something worth living for. And as someone who spent much of his life idle and wandering, evading the draft and rarely working, he was an unlikely American hero. Tracy was showing Natalie a drawing he'd done that summer of the gendarme's booth in Luxembourg Gardens. I decided not to mention a connection that occurred to me between John Muir and Mark Twain: they both hated Indians.

I walked alone down College Avenue, and when I stepped into Kyla's apartment all the lights were out. I knew she was home, but she wasn't in bed and the bathroom door was closed. I called her name and she didn't answer. When I opened the bathroom door I heard her breathe slightly. I looked in, and there she was, in the tub, her wet hair pulled in front of her face, staring at the wall.

"You all right?" I asked.

She shook her head in the darkness—no. But no idea why not. None. Just a knot of objectless guilt. I turned on all the lights in the place and faked hilarity, waltzed her naked through the apartment. But I couldn't make her laugh and regretted trying. Dripping naked on the hardwood floor, her shoulders slumped, she said she felt numb all over, especially in her brain.

Twenty-six

"It's the darkness," Kyla said triumphantly, sipping a pint of Caramel Alt at a local brewpub, "that willingness to just say 'fuck it.'" She shook her hair back in defiance like a male model on a runway as she described what it was I didn't have. Hectic, squalid Berkeley was getting her down and she wanted adventure. We were going climbing together the next day, but that wasn't at all what she had in mind— she wanted to invite a woman into our lovemaking. As I watched her spin a silver ring around and around on her middle finger, I thought how shocked my buddies would be if I refused. I tried to get excited by picturing positions, but clearly the point was really for her to have sex with other people and keep me around. The female combination was apparently meant as a panacea—appeasing both my jealousy and homophobia; pleasure without loss.

"I'd feel left out," I said, "I know it."

On an enormous old British motorcycle another of her current preoccupations arrived for work at the bar. He wore the latest illiterate rebel poet's uniform—black leather jacket and boots, ponytail and John Lennon glasses, Levis so shredded that decency demanded long johns.

"I let you climb your mountains," she said, watching the biker take off his leather. "Why can't I climb some of my own?"

"You're kidding, right?"

"What's the big deal? I still love you."

I did an instant replay to make sure I wasn't hearing things, then took a good look at her to make sure she was serious. As she sipped her pint, her eyes followed the creep around the room.

"You're just really into goals," she told me. She ran her ring-clustered fingers through her hair. "I think I'm more into experience. I mean, I totally love being with you, so don't take this personally, but you are really, really conservative." I was stunned. Conservative? For not wanting group sex and an open relationship? I watched the biker hang up his leather jacket and put on an apron. He had a wave tattooed on his pale, slender arm.

"I think it's a pretty standard provision in human mating contracts," I said. "No outside fucking." The rebel poet cut into a tomato with a serrated knife.

"You're so vulgar," she said. "Loosen up."

I guessed I needed to, I mean, maybe I was being a little uptight. But was it his bad skin? The earring? His speed habit? Anyone can buy a jacket and smoke. Takes no balls at all to drink midday, but the guy did have a certain roguish sexiness about him, and I was increasingly wearing asexual outdoorsy clothes. Red hair and glasses are pretty hard to make look brooding.

Inadequacy loomed. I made a last bid. "How can you see him as reckless?!" I asked, sitting up straight. "I spend whole weeks in the mountains, drinking around fires with unemployed men. I do shit so ballsy on rocks he'd peepee in his chaps." I looked at the guy again, knowing he had me. "He just turns an accelerator on a factory-made metal cock and you think he's reckless! Who's reckless?"

"Don't worry," Kyla said, smiling broadly and leaning to kiss me, "you're a man."

Twenty-seven

"What do I hold on to!?" Kyla screamed. She lay against the rock and looked down at the manzanita on the ground, a hundred feet below. I saw her shoulders quiver with sobs. Her left foot slipped an inch and she shrieked. I pulled up on the rope from above.

"Relax," I said, "you can't fall anywhere because of the rope."

"This isn't fun," she declared, her face streaming with tears, "and I can't just relax."

She looked at me sixty feet above where I was tied into a tree at the top of the cliff. Then she looked along the wall of Lover's Leap in both directions and back to the Pony Express Trail below where a man and a little boy were eating lunch. I pulled harder on the rope.

"You know," I said, "there's a . . . just above your right arm there's a pretty big hold, yeah. Now, try to . . . "

"Shut up." She put her hands on the big hold above her and pulled up. Her feet started slipping until all of her weight was on her arms. I could see her hands turning red and her thin biceps quivering. The little boy was watching us.

"Do you want an idea for the next move?"

She just glared: this, for love.

When she got near the top, I reached down to help.

"Don't touch me." She climbed up and walked away from the edge. She stood facing me, knees and elbows skinned, gray T-shirt wet with sweat, her eyes bloodshot. "That was a crappy experience," she said. "In fact, I think it's sick that you enjoy this."

As we walked silently down from the route, kicking through dirt and pebbles below the cliff, we heard yelling up ahead. A hundred feet off the ground a frizzy-haired woman in a purple windbreaker and biking shorts stood on a small ledge screaming. Her male partner had led far above and was calling down at her, demanding she climb. She cried back that she couldn't. Unable to hear or see her, he yelled again and pulled on the rope while she clutched at the rock. She looked down, then up, then tried the first move off the ledge, and couldn't do it. She tried again, then again, then went back to whimpering.

Two women who'd been eating French bread and cheddar cheese on the boulders below racked up and started climbing toward her. While they led up to her perch, the man above kept hollering down in this deep, scratchy voice and hauling on the rope. When the first of the women climbers reached the ledge—a long-haired brunette in canvas pants, she set up an anchor and clipped the stranded woman into it amidst thanks, hugs and tears. Just before the stranded one began rappelling back to the ground, the brunette untied her from the man's rope. The guy yelled indignantly for her to climb again, apparently with no idea that she was being helped. Once the rope was untied, the brunette gave it a strong yank, and let go of it. Its now weightless loose end suddenly zipped upwards, the clueless man clearly in a panic, imagining that his lover had fallen to a grisly death.

Moments later he came running down the path with gear piled all over him. A tan, lanky man with close-set dark eyes, he had the rope in a medusa coil around his shoulders. As he and his partner walked sullenly off into the woods, the rescuer winked at Kyla and said,

"Guess they won't be zipping the ol' bags together tonight, huh?"

Back at the car, packing to leave, Kyla was silent.

Afraid I'd blown it, ruined a chance of our doing this together, I said again and again that I thought she could be great at climbing—so flexible and such balance. As we drove through the American River canyon, I explained how women can pick up climbing better than men, that upper-body strength's really not what it's about. I told her she moved beautifully and insisted we'd been on a very difficult route. I told her how much I'd love to have her along on all of my road trips, how the man-thing got old quickly and how many times when Nick and I had been sitting in some spectacular hot spring, all alone, we'd politely inquired if the other would mind changing sex.

"Dan," Kyla said, "I got into the farm."

Out of the canyon, we passed development on a scale approaching southern California. The corridor from Tahoe to Sacramento, Sacramento to the Bay Area, seemed to change weekly. Housing tracts spread away from the highway.

"Big Sur?"

"Yeah."

About two hundred miles south of Berkeley. "For how long?"

"I don't know. A year?" She looked at her hands. The rock had torn up her knuckles.

"Just up and going?"

"I could probably come home on weekends, and you could come down whenever you want. I'm going to live in a tent." Her parents wouldn't believe it. They'd been disgusted enough by her hairy legs and armpits.

"Couldn't you learn the same stuff in Berkeley? Or somewhere nearby?"

"It's more about the forest," she said, "you know? I want to be in a small community in a small place."

Back in town, her friends Christopher and Naomi La Salle stopped by on the way to the same Big Sur farm. They'd been living up in Arcata in Humboldt County making jewelry but Naomi was pregnant and they wanted to get experience to start a farm of their own. Naomi had just finished a degree in Herstory at Humboldt State—an interdisciplinary major in History and Women's Studies. A kind, vulnerable young woman from a wealthy San Francisco suburb, she'd been Kyla's best friend until high school. She had shiny, curly black hair and very pale, fresh skin with freckles on her nose and chest. Once she got seated comfortably with her swollen belly, she offered a leather necklace to Kyla. It had a crystal hanging from a ring of silver, and Naomi said it was to celebrate their coming time together on the farm.

"In a funny way, crystals control the world," Naomi said, almost begging us with her eyes to believe. "I mean, silicon chips are crystals, just without the oxygen. We were making necklaces and bracelets with them, usually out of leather. Some people prefer synthetic bands though, cause they're cruelty-free."

Christopher was in his early thirties and though physically he looked his age, his presence felt older. His olive skin was rutted and worn. He had high cheekbones and a thin, delicate nose. Crow's feet spread away from his dark green eyes and shadows underlined them as if after decades of trust-funded bacchanalia the tragedy of his little life had begun to occur to him. He seemed both to look forward to the baby and to be exhausted by the thought. He wore three loose silver bracelets on his wrist and had a fading tattoo of a snake wrapped around his right forearm. His loose black tank top exposed his too-tan, elegant collar-bones. He said he'd grown up in Puerto Vallarta, where his French mother still lived. In fact it reminded him he owed her a visit.

"I think the cruelty thing's bullshit," he said. "You honor the cow by using its whole body." Kyla poured nettle tea into bowls and sat down on the floor near Christopher. She smiled at me in a way either pitying or apologetic—I couldn't decide. Chris talked on:

"I've been reading about decay and regeneration and how synthetic materials just contribute to the big death." He stopped to sip at his tea and Naomi said, "Anyway, the leather on yours, Ky, was all from sacred cows in India that died of old age."

Kyla and I stood in the street and watched them drive off in their enormous old school bus. I wondered aloud what motivated people to buy such ridiculous machines. Back inside, Kyla and I made more tea and looked at each other across the floor for a while. She laughed a little about how scared she'd been on the rocks, and I tried half-heartedly to talk her out of the farm. I knew I shouldn't, that I should let go, but I had a feeling I'd lose her altogether. Her affections were so ephemeral as it was. As we got into bed together she cuddled up against my back and whispered in my ear, "I want to compost."

Twenty-eight

Thieves, fools and madmen on Telegraph Avenue: Mr. Surge shrieked fractal geometry at passersby while university bulldozers closed in on People's Park. The hunchback of South Berkeley picked through latte cups in a dumpster and the street poet/bubble lady sold her books to tourists who loved the idea. Looking for a used *Huckleberry Finn*, I bumped into Aaron Lehrman in front of Moe's Books. Out of the blue, there he was—six-foot-four and sunburned, with his almost-white hair grown out into a ponytail. Blond stubble on his goofy, round, beaming face; he'd come shuffling down the street in laceless old basketball shoes, cut-off black sweatpants and a T-shirt with a picture of a screaming woman swinging on a ceiling light fixture over her appalled psychologist's couch, captioned "Jung and the Restless." Last I'd heard from his mom he'd been working as a ranch hand in Wyoming.

"Oh, Jesus, Dan," he said, scratching his head and looking up the street when I asked him about it, "so embarrassing. Falling off horses, lassoing the wrong cow. I actually bailed for Alaska instead. Almost drowned working on a fishing boat, tramped around Denali for a while. Shitty weather. People dying everywhere." He nodded and wiped his nose with his thumb and finger. "Yeah, no kidding. It's weird seeing guys on the mountain, and then the next day they die a thousand feet above you. Six people died while we were there. It was eery." He'd filled out since I'd last seen him, but still had his sloped-shouldered bouncing gait.

"You want to go climbing?" I asked. God, I wanted to do something huge.

"Yeah. When? Weekends are bad for me."

"Why, what do you do weekends?"

"Climb."

"Oh, well how about next week? All week?" I asked.

"Yeah."

"Want to do a Big Wall?" Nick'd be bummed.

"Yeah," he said, "let's do the Nose."

"Fuck no."

"Half Dome?"

"Look, how about Washington Column?"

"Yeah."

"You know the route?"

"No. Never heard of it."

"Ever done a wall?"

"No. Be nice to snooze on a ledge, though, huh?"

Sunday night when I left the mountain shop, my gear was already packed. I filled the duct-taped water bottles and called for a pizza; I asked whether thin or thick crust would hold up best.

"What are you going to do with it?" the man asked.

"Haul it up a cliff in Yosemite, eat it on a ledge. It's got to have some structural integrity."

"Just a minute," he said, "let me grab someone who'd know more about this." A moment later a reedy-voiced woman picked up the phone.

"Ok," she said, "what route are you doing?"

I picked up the deep dish with artichoke hearts and hit the road. Off to do a big wall—Big Wall. Sleep on a ledge, wake up in the morning still on the route, try outrageously serious techniques like aid climbing where you place gear and actually pull up on it, pendulum swings where you run horizontally across the wall. On the rock for two straight days. Forty-eight hours' hard work in the sky. Phenomenal. I'd borrowed my dad's Half Dome equipment, his hallowed old jumar mechanical rope ascenders and nylon aid stirrups.

At 10:00 p.m. sharp I pulled into the parking lot of the Ahwahnee Hotel and saw Aaron sitting on a bench eating Froot Loops from a box. A janitor was running around inside trying to track down plastic garbage bags for Aaron to use in place of the rain gear he'd left in someone's car. He'd been working on the design for a few hours—had it wired when the bags arrived.

Late into the night we packed our haul bag—an old army duffle—with food, sleeping bags, warm clothing, water. At a gallon each per day, planning for two days, and eight pounds per gallon, we had forty-eight pounds of water alone. In the morning, long before dawn, Aaron yawned once, pulled on his sneakers, and swung the enormous eighty-pound beast onto his back like a knapsack.

We moved fast through the forest to the thousand-foot pillar called Washington Column. A lovely, rounded ship's prow of granite, it looked up at the omnipresent massif of Half Dome. If we did everything right, we'd be off the ground until the following night. What a concept. No retreat to terra plata at the end of the day, no bullshit session in the bar. No beers and burritos around a fire.

After a miserable bushwacking, knee-scraping slog up eroding slopes and granite slabs, hardware and ropes wrapped all over my aching body, we reached the base of the route. We got off the ground quickly, but the haul bag was another matter. After thrashing the miserably heavy pig around for a hundred feet it blew two holes the size of silver dollars. But by eleven-thirty, we were safely at Dinner Ledge where we'd spend the night—a big, comfortable terrace with a panoramic view of the valley. Our plan was to climb three more pitches that night, hang ropes on them, then rappel back to the ledge to eat and sleep. Then we'd jet up our ropes in the morning to get a head start on the next day's work.

The classic first big wall. After the East Buttress of El Cap, Dad had called the Column the next big step; a sort of initiation route before Half Dome, the place to learn all the complicated techniques and sort out kinks in your system. He said efficiency and tenacity were of the essence. Only if I could keep it together on the Column could I consider Half Dome; the Dome was more than twice as big and in

many ways much harder. But if we could get up Half Dome
without any major epics, given our youth, he thought we
could start thinking about El Cap, maybe.

Off to the side of the main ledge were a few smaller
terraces—one with a good-sized tree on it and some shade.
While we ate sourdough French bread Aaron talked about
hoboing on trains up to Northern California to pick apples
with migrant workers. His dad, mystified but impressed by
his son's wanderings, had offered to pay the bus fare. But
Aaron said you can't catch busses up to do that kind of
work. You got to hop trains.

I draped my sleeping bag over a manzanita to shade
the anchor. Half Dome loomed in the haze of thousands of
morning campfires; a vague, gray half-circle reaching thousands of feet overhead and filling most of the southeastern
sky like one of those global space ships in old comic books.
Aaron racked up and started climbing toward the big overhang. He wasted no time at all, and while I stretched out on
packs and clothes, he moved easily to the base of the Kor
Roof. It stuck out at least ten feet from the wall and had
bolts drilled all the way to its lip. Aaron clipped aiders onto
the bolts and stepped out into them. With his feet in the
aiders, he hung completely free of the rock and swung
around in the wind over an awfully long drop below.

He seemed confused and slow at first; the reach out to
each bolt took a long time, and he had to fight with the
equipment to keep it untangled. At one point he dangled
horizontally in his harness while he wrestled off his shirt. It
finally came drifting down to me, then right on past to the

forest below. He seemed gaunt from his time in Alaska, but his arms had become those of a weight lifter. He worked from one bolt to the next, and eventually found a rhythm. No flailing aiders whipping around his head, no collapsing in his harness like I'd heard guys talk about. Aaron just did it and yelled down he didn't know what the big deal was.

He built an anchor, then attached the rope to it so I could ascend with the jumars rather than reclimbing the bolts. As I prepared to follow I could see Aaron dangling directly overhead, pushing himself out from the wall, spreading his arms wide and laughing to himself. No idea I was watching him. Ascending up the roof, I kept taking wild, nauseating swings out from the wall—each time I unclipped the rope from a bolt, it would drop my weight into the air. When each spin stopped I was hanging well below the next bolt, and had to repeat the fall. My sweaty palms slipped around on the jumar handles. Directly behind, Half Dome loomed. Three more disgusting, horrifying swings and I had turned the roof.

We swapped leads for two more pitches—long, grueling aid cracks with the sun turning a few clouds into the pastel pinks of a Caribbean dusk. Shadows spread out in sharp, horizontal lines across the wall as the stone around us began to glow yellow. Aaron led the final aid pitch of the day, and I had all the time in the world to hang there in my harness, high above the valley on clean, warm granite and watch the sun ease into the darkening foothills.

When we'd gone as far as we could for the day, we rappelled fast over the now crimson cliff. My hand burned from the friction. We hit Dinner Ledge with legs sore, arms cramping, skin shaved off knees and knuckles; Aaron grinned with pure, childish delight and opened up the pizza. Finally exhausted enough to feel relaxed. Deep-dish with artichoke hearts and long, spacy looks up at Half Dome still orange in the sun's last light. I remembered again the light of my father's Half Dome pictures—he and Sean happily fatigued in that same orange glow.

"Dan!" Aaron whispered. I jolted awake, noticed an absurd number of stars overhead. "It's the wall beast!"

"What?!"

"There!"

Something scurried away. "I don't believe it," Aaron said, largely to himself. "I swear I saw two red dots staring at me!"

At first light I opened my eyes and discovered how sore, sick to my stomach, stiff and sweat-caked I was. The inside of my sleeping bag was sticky, rancid and heavenly. My throbbing hands were so puffed-up and scabbed they looked gangrenous. From the gravel next to my head, our fixed rope stretched up out into a granite-gray sky. Aaron sat up and yawned, with dirt smeared across his face and his hands black with aluminum oxide. He declined the compressed, misshapen bran muffin I'd brought for him and started up the rope back to our high point.

With the ropes hanging away from the rock, jumaring up over the roofs just about finished both of us. Herculean efforts, all-out oxygen debt and flailing wrestling matches got me a few feet at a time. Coffee and scrambled eggs at the deli sounded fine, but I hadn't the vaguest idea how to bail even if I'd decided to. I'd imagined it as "Wake up before dawn, jam up the lines, be on the summit by noon." That's the way everyone always talked about jumaring—like it took five minutes per pitch and was practically motorized.

In one of my exhausted rotating pauses, I looked up and laughed out loud. I realized I'd arrived—all those great old photographs of climbers jumaring in space at dawn on the Wall of the Early Morning Light, of Yvonne Chouinard on North America Wall. Away off west, stretching above the Three Brothers, the Dawn Wall itself was actually catching that first gentle light. I hung for a while, rotating, empty of the mundane, full of the commonplace: small arrivals. I rested my head for a while against a patch of granite.

At the belay, Aaron giggled with nervous exhaustion.

"What a breeze, huh dude? Just jet up those fixed lines? You know, bomb right up 'em?"

In shade or wind the heat was tolerable, but exposed I felt my pale skin burning, getting tighter. Long vertical aid cracks and hard free-climbing went beautifully. The day drifted by and before sunset we made it out of a rotten, crumbling gully to the summit. We stood together on a broad platform of stone. Done. I was very tired, but not nearly like I'd expected. Aaron started coiling ropes—going about his business. I dropped the gear hanging all over me and just sat down to stare for a while at the mountains all around.

"Hey, Dan . . . "

"Yeah?"

"What's this thing look like?"

"What thing?"

"The Column."

"What do you mean? You just climbed it."

"Yeah, but I never got a good look at the whole thing. Pretty cool-looking?"

Twenty-nine

"On to the Nose, huh?" Aaron said, looking out from the summit of the Column. A Jeffrey pine rooted amidst manzanita leaned out over him while he repacked the shredded haul bag; you've got to respect manzanita; it takes no lip. You can try to finesse your way through it all you want—it'll catch skin somewhere and tear it.

I begged to differ: "The Nose is like three times the size and way harder." Just the thought made me nervous. And I'd actually done a lot more rock climbing than he.

"Ah, that's all bullshit. You're ready. We gotta do big routes."

Thanks, but no thanks. He'd torn one of his knees near the end of the route; dried blood mingled with dirt was caked clear down to his foot. "Picking apples up north ain't easy," he said out of the blue, then looked away.

"No?"

"Nope. That's hard work. Time you get up till it's too dark to pick, you pick apples for twenty bucks a day. Like two bucks an hour. But Reed College was driving me nuts. That place is kind of bullshit."

"How long'd you last picking?"

"Couple days."

"Hop a train back?"

"Almost. I hitched back to the freight yard. And I kind of slunk around until this big yard cop asked me where I was going. Big muscly guy, really mean-looking. Had a gun and a little clipboard. You always got to watch out for guys with clipboards." Aaron got a huge, bare foot into the bag now to pack down our sleeping bags. He hopped up and down on them as he talked. "I was spooked," he said, between hops, "but also kind of out of it, so I just told him. I can't lie to anybody. He looks at me really close, squinting kind of, then he looks at the clipboard and goes, 'track 11, leaves in fifteen minutes, stay in the rear boxes.' Turned out to be a train for Tracy, and I wasn't sure where Tracy was so I called my mom and she wired me money for the bus."

Aaron shouldered the haul bag again while I draped our three ropes and mass of hardware around my shoulders. Even with that ridiculous weight on him he walked upright, as though the bag were empty—the physics just didn't seem to add up. Then we started walking, picking our way along the valley rim. Enough light remained to make the dangerous part of the descent feasible. The path went through manzanita tunnels and over slabs to the top of the column, then along the valley rim above the column's east face, above Astroman and Mideast Crisis. Climbers' feet had worn it to a washed-out, eroding sand track with sucker's trails leading off every ten feet. To the left, the uphill side, they'd been formed by the nervous, unsure of the way and not liking being on loose dirt twenty or thirty feet from a five-hundred-foot drop; they'd take you wandering safely but aimlessly up toward North Dome.

To the right, through the trees and scrub, other little tracks led quickly to dirt too loose and steep for good footing, then to a long, long fall. Straight ahead the path crossed smooth, down-sloping slabs of mottled granite, dropped among branches and roots where trees grew right up along the slope, then through oddly perched little clumps of forest.

Aaron started talking again as the soaring east face of the column came into view to our right.

"Ranching actually paid awesomely," he said. "That's what got me to Alaska. Ranch hands are nuts. Campfires every night out there with hordes of beer and this big ladder up over the fire for ranting if you had to rant."

The angle had eased, and we could let ourselves along by holding on to tree limbs. Deep, clean dihedrals leaned up across the wall.

"Went out with one of these guys to this wild spot down in Utah called the Maze. You drive like ten miles on this four-wheel-drive jeep track out there, banging around . . . ten miles took us hours."

Aaron half-ran, half-stumbled ahead of me through a clump of trees, grabbing their thin trunks and swinging around them as he hopped down the badly worn trail. "We started in with our packs and everything," he said as we emerged again onto slabs. I had to stop for a moment to tie a shoe. "It's these canyons all over the place and there's only two ways in without rappelling and they're about four miles apart. Just walking around down in these gorgeous, deep canyons with more canyons branching off all over the place in different directions and all of them look exactly the same.

"So we were out there looking for this spring, because we forgot water, and finally at the end of the day we found it. Well, it turned out we'd kind of spaced the whole food issue too."

"You walked off backpacking in the desert without food or water?"

He looked a little embarrassed and rubbed the top of his head. "We were kind of stoned," he said, apologetically. "But we did have a bag of pot brownies and a can of jalapeños. Man, it was so hot."

"Jalapeños?"

"I know. They were pretty hot too. But we were in the desert. You got to eat that kind of stuff in the desert."

The pain of my sore muscles, sunburnt skin, raw, swollen and too-moist feet, buckling knees and the welts forming on my shoulders from the ropes all fused into a kind of low hum, a nonverbal mantra that kept me abstracted, tuned-out as we hopped down successive shelves of granite.

"We pretty much passed out for the night," Aaron yelled back up at me, having gotten too far ahead for convenient storytelling. His knees were indestructible. "It's intense down there," he said, shaking his head and looking around in the darkening treetops. "Totally still. We woke up feeling pretty spaced and hungry. So we ate a few pot brownies for breakfast. We needed the calories. And anyway, we still wanted to poke around. Beautiful walls, incredible geology. This guy I was with was a geologist. Intense to see the whole thing, but I wasn't sure I bought it."

"Geology?" I could feel the sickening slipperiness of silver-dollar-sized blisters forming on the balls of both feet. The sun had set behind the Valley walls; twilight softened shadows and deepened the forest darkness. I saw nothing in the forest at times like that, slamming ahead with a purpose, watching the trail and making a racket.

"Yeah," Aaron mumbled, still talking away. "It was cool to see how rocks are actually moving. The whole scientific vision, but that's just one vision. Like, I almost saw a spirit in a rock."

"Not quite though, huh?"

"Almost." He paused. We were beneath a famous climb called Astroman.

"Just for that moment," Aaron said, "I thought I could see more than a random process. It was gone pretty fast though. Science is a downer. It was so hot down there. And we kept walking around, not much idea where we were." He stopped.

"Kind of lost?"

"Well, I don't know, pretty spaced-out though. We found this waterfall overlooking the Colorado, and splashed around in it. You could see like all the way down to the river. It was great. We just hung out and had pot brownies for dinner."

"How many brownies did you bring?" My enfeebled mind was trying to do the math, failing.

"A lot."

"How many?"

"Kind of a lot of brownies. Pretty much a grocery bag."

"Getting pretty out of it by this point?"

"We needed the calories, and they were tasting amazing. Really sweet. So the next morning we woke up and had some pot brownies for breakfast and started walking. At the end of that day we found our own footsteps in some sand by a dry creek."

"Walking in circles?"

"Sort of, but when we found our footprints we knew where we were. Man, if it had rained and washed out our tracks . . . whew. But we knew we had about fourteen miles to go, and it was just getting dark. So we ate some pot brownies and started walking. We had to get out of there. Walked all night. Brutally jamming along for like eight hours. We got back to the road at dawn and searched the whole car for something to eat."

"Nothing?"

"Nowhere."

"Nowhere in the entire car?"

"Nope."

"Not in the whole entire car, nothing to eat?"

"Except a six-pack of Bud."

"So you drank it?"

"Needed the calories. So we each had a few beers, then started driving. Yeah, and we still had to get past the dirt road. Oh, it was brutal, slamming up and down, bouncing off the ceiling, almost cracking axles. But when we hit the highway we were psyched. Hollering shit out the windows. Going nuts."

"Blazing along?"

"No way. We kept it right at fifty-five. We didn't want to get pulled over. We had a lot of dope in the car. We could've been busted."

"Exactly how much dope did you have?"

"Kind of a lot. So we come around this corner and can't believe our eyes—a Utah State Trooper highway drug check. Unbelievable. No way we could just turn around and blaze. Too obvious. So we waited with the other cars, and then this fat trooper came up. Psyched to bust us. I'm telling you, there was pot all over the car."

"Everywhere?"

"Everywhere. And, like, we had kind of spaced on concealing it very well. It was just in paper shopping bags."

"Shopping bags?"

"We had a lot of pot. But Dan, don't think I'm really into drugs or anything. I almost never smoke pot. It makes me too sleepy. It was all this other guy's. So, anyway, the trooper finally made it to our car. Fat Mormon. We looked pretty weird. Nothing but pot brownies for three days in the desert. And jalapeños. And Bud. So the trooper looked in at me and said, 'Where you boys been?' and there we were. Me and this trooper. I'm exactly the scum he's looking for and I look exactly like that scum is supposed to look. Tan as hell. Grizzled. Weirdo kaleidoscope eyes and a stupid expression on my face in a dusty off-road vehicle. He could just smell the sin. So he asks again, 'Where you boys been?' and I looked back at him right in his squinty, dark little eyes and said, 'Desert.' He kept looking at me. Squinting. After a long time, he said, 'Huh.'

"He asked for the registration, and I opened up the glove compartment, and man . . . "

"Buds?"

"A big bag of sticky green ones. So, I palmed it and handed him the registration. Miracle he didn't catch it. Really, Dan, it's not like I'm some big druggy."

We were directly below the column now, on another faint trail of loose, sliding dirt and rocks.

"So he poked around the car for a reason to search it. I guess they can't actually search without a probable cause, but that can probably be anything, like bad registration or a turn signal out. He went through everything. They had dogs checking out another car. They would've smelled the pot for sure and we would have been screwed. California plates . . . we could have been busted for being dealers." Aaron stumbled suddenly under the weight of the bag, then caught himself on a tree limb.

"We had kind of a lot of pot," he continued, standing still for a moment. "The whole car stank like a road-kill Indica skunk. Trooper came back from doing the computer check really slow. He came up to the window looking pissed. 'Well,' he said, like leaning inside and looking around like he's about to lay us into the Utah Gulag for life with serial jaywalkers and other psychotics, when he says, 'I can't find anything wrong with anything, so I guess I'm going to have to let you boys go. Drive carefully.' Shocking. We went straight for burgers. I had a great time out there, Dan."

"Out in the desert, huh?"

"Out in the desert."

We were sliding along the trail and hopping down big lichen-covered boulders in the dark. Half Dome still glowed high above with the evening that had long since left the valley floor. At last we made it to the road, and the pavement had an alien flatness and firmness. In the warmth rising out of the asphalt we ambled along the yellow dividing line back to the Ahwahnee lot. Six Honda Goldwing touring motorcycles cooled off next to my truck. Six couples in matching leather jumpsuits were just walking into the hotel.

Thirty

A shrieking blue jay woke me up, my skin and sleeping bag for once dry and clean. Damp green redwood forest hung over the wooden platform that supported Kyla's yellow tent; high leaves scattered sunlight across our morning and down the overgrown hillside to the little farm below. Under the tent's netting I lay and listened and waited for Kyla to wake up. She was curled against my side with her face under the covers, trying to sleep in, perfectly happy to let time slip by while she lay in bed. I couldn't imagine being able to relax like that, and could never decide whether her serenity wasn't part inertia; she seemed so at home wrapped up in nylon and down.

Kyla'd been disgusted the night before by the scabs all over my hands and the apparently infected swelling; now I could see what she meant. I had lousy, red, wrinkled skin on my hands even when they were healthy. Our sleeping bags were zipped together, and they were full of her smell—sweat, patchouli, and some herb she'd been chewing. A woodpecker rattled away nearby; large mosquitos patrolled the outside of the netting. On the tent floor I noticed the crystal Naomi had given Kyla, broken. Kyla had insisted it jumped out of her hand by itself. While I played with the redder hair that grew beneath Kyla's sun-bleached blond—all of it electric across her bright blue sleeping bag—the sun seemed suddenly to fade out. Bright colors and gleaming dew quickly dulled. A finger of mist distinct as a ghost filtered down from the hill above—fog blown in from the ocean soon dripped off the ancient redwoods like the softest of rains. Sword ferns and bay trees shone wet.

Kyla'd be furious if I woke her, so I stepped out onto the wooden platform and stretched, tried to figure out the scene I'd walked through the night before. Leading away from the platform, a footpath threaded between patches of poison oak down to the valley of the farm. My fingers still smelled of bay from pulling on branches as I'd walked up in the dark. When I reached back into the tent for my jeans, Kyla opened her eyes and stared at me.

"Isn't this pretty?" she asked softly. She sat up on her elbows and looked out into the trees. "I get the best sleeps here."

"Slept pretty well on that ledge with Aaron," I told her. She shuddered at the thought, as if the whole project were a sign of emotional imbalance. I asked her to tell me about her first week on the farm, whether it had been hard work.

"We played Earthlove yesterday," she said, falling back down and looking up at the trees. "It was amazing." She put on long johns, a purple Guatemalan coarse wool sweater, and black nylon river sandals, and we picked our way down the path to the valley. We ambled along a dirt road with a small creek barely running on one side and an acre of broccoli growing on the other. Beyond the broccoli were the tents of three more interns and a dirt basketball court with a tractor rusting beneath the hoop. The fog thickened overhead and beaded up on Kyla's sweater and hair. All around the farm were brambled mountainsides, their peaks lost in the gray marine mist.

Beyond a small, fenced-off herb garden we walked up the porch of the little, dark green group house. Inside, the air was cold and the raw plank floors creaked under us. In the kitchen, with kerosene burning next to stained-glass windows, Kyla mixed a tea of gota-kola, damiana, stevia and kawa kawa in a pot of boiling water—brain tonic, male tonic/aphrodisiac, sweetener, and dream enhancer. She yawned—worn-out from planting seedlings—and leaned her face against me. I asked her to tell me more about the game with the great name and she stood upright.

"Earthlove's from this place called Findhorn up in Scotland," she said, shaking back her hair and glowing with the thought. "I seriously have to go. This totally motherly, witchpower, awesome woman told us about it."

I was almost certain I'd heard the poetry editor mention Findhorn once. In fact, I thought he'd been there. But I couldn't remember his take on it.

"It's like a farm up in the arctic circle," she explained, "where they grow tropical fruits and stuff, and all these scientists can't explain it. This woman's the one who prays to the plant devas. You think I'm nuts, Dan, but this stuff's going to be hip soon. Watch. Mainstream America's going to catch on."

In the other room I could see Shari, a calm but frightened woman, drinking tea and reading *Ecowarriors*. Her face, covered in an herbal mud mask, glowed yellow in the candlelight. On the altar beside her were feathers from many birds. A bronze sculpture of a nude woman sitting akimbo had crystal eyes; its belly was huge and open, filled with shards of rose-quartz in a symmetrical cosmos. Drums lay about the altar. Smoke rose from a small brass urn and the smell of burning sage drifted into the kitchen.

"What about *this* farm?" I asked.

"Let me tell you about the game first." She placed a few drops from an echinacea tincture onto her tongue, shivered, and said, "I know it's sudden, but this woman changed my life, I think. I'm not kidding." She smiled to herself, apparently charmed by her own caprice. She poured the tea through a bamboo strainer into wooden bowls. Its sweet and complex smell steamed up into the sage smoke. I followed her into the room with the altar. Three nights before I'd slept on a cliff; two nights before in an urban apartment; the night before with Kyla, warm and welcoming but again preoccupied even as she'd rubbed my back with olive oil.

The candles pushed shadows of the ceiling beams into shaking patterns and a dog barked in the fog outside. On the plank walls hung tapestries and blankets. Layer upon layer of Asian, Latin American and Native American rugs dampened sound from the floor. We sat close together on pillows by a wood-burning stove in a corner.

"People have started going there," Kyla said.

Scotland? I tried to remember that maxim about culti-
vating one's own garden, but couldn't.

Shari overheard, looked up and smiled lightly. "It's on
a line of convergence," she said, in all seriousness.

"So's Ithaca, New York," I offered. Aaron had told me
that Mounts Aconcagua, Shasta, Rainier and Denali were
too. For some reason Kyla still made me want to shed my
reflexive disbelief. She didn't quite seem deluded or gull-
ible; it was more like she'd made a decision not to be ham-
pered by self-consciousness. She talked about the spiral
dance of creation like one story in a vacuum, but one story
she'd chosen.

"How about around here?" I asked again, wanting to
hear some agriculture talk. It didn't look bad at all, in fact it
reminded me of places my parents had taken the family on
summer vacations in the early seventies. The funnest one
of all—a big farming community started by neighbors of
ours—had produced one of California's most notorious
serial killers. But while it lasted, my sister and I had whole
blazing hot summers of skinny dipping in the murky water
hole and bouncing around in old pickups with local teenagers.

"No listen. You pick a marker that's like a familiar—
different amulets and crystals, rocks . . . anything that has
meaning to you. I got a cinnamon stick. Isn't that perfect
for me? It totally ties in with my all of my loves—it's an
herb, it's a cooking spice, it's a bark which is like trees, it
smells like food . . . "

"And I love cinnamon toast," I added, "always have."

"Right, right. Exactly, jerk." She looked down into the steam of her bowl and braids fell around her face. She'd shed a few earrings, and just like Aaron and I on the column, looked fatigued but rested. The game did sound a little funny to me, but it also sounded pretty real; I wouldn't mind getting back to the garden myself. And Kyla certainly wasn't going to let cheap cynicism keep her from that preindustrial place in the heart where she wanted to live.

"Then you choose an ally out of a deck of cards. Actually . . . it chooses you. I got the bear, and we realized it was because of the bear's fierce love of family." She leaned forward and said quietly, so Shari wouldn't hear, "It's also hilarious, because it brought me back to all the teddy bears I had when I was little. I had a family of koala bears and I felt bad because I couldn't sleep with all of them every night, so I made a chart so they could rotate and take turns so no one would get hurt. Kind of like living at Barrington in college.

"So then we rolled dice and entered the mineral kingdom and I got to thinking about Chris and Naomi in Berkeley that time, and how the crystal she gave me jumped out of my hand and broke. They've got a great house here, by the way."

The fire died down again, and I stoked it. Shari read on in *Ecowarriors*, looking concerned. Kyla continued.

"So then you had to decide whether you wanted consciousness beads, which were clear stones, or teardrops, which were blue stones. I chose three rocks for grounding because I give too much."

"How's that?" I asked, genuinely curious.

"Just to the world. I know I'm weird about giving to

you, but I really do give too much love to the world and feel too much pain. It's why I don't read newspapers."

The wooden door latch slid open, moved from the outside. Hog, an enormous, dying German shepherd, walked in. A small man, bearded and cheerful, came after him and left the door open. He smiled and took off his work boots. Sun had cut through the fog and lit up the porch while the fields beyond were still gray and obscure. With its rough-cut, weathered boards, the porch looked like the place on our neighbors' big farm where my dad had started teaching me to play bluegrass guitar. Our family's momentary Arcadia—just brief enough to be worth remembering.

"Got this great chicken," the bearded man said. "Down at the meat place in town you can get these chickens that don't eat any hormones or chemicals and they don't raise them in little boxes." Kyla didn't respond. Nor did Shari. He walked across the carpet and into the kitchen.

"Bugs the shit out of me," Kyla whispered. "He says the most obvious things. And like rants forever about what bullshit the government is, which it is, but it gets so boring. He thinks he's the first person in the world to know about hormones and pesticides."

Pots clanged in the kitchen. The bearded man told Hog to at least try to eat.

"Anyway, he actually landed on magician, so he could do anything he wanted, like send the whole class on a walk or say everyone has to sing a song. He said we had to choose from a tarot deck."

Hog's master came back into the room and sat down next to Shari. He started telling her how much better the organic chicken tastes than that stuff with all the chemical crap in it from the supermarket. Kyla lowered her voice and kept talking.

"The first card I pulled was the Death card." She smiled and took a deep drink of tea.

"Isn't that terrible?" I asked. I imagined an axe-wielding, cloaked horseman.

"No, not at all. You can see it as like 'end of an era,' and then I got Chariot, and then reverse Empress."

I figured Chariot meant she was going somewhere, but before I could ask about reverse Empress, the front door opened again. A man in his twenties with bushy dark hair entered smiling a small, tight, butler's smile. He sat down on a couch nearby with his knees and feet close together and his hands in his lap and nodded to me. His name was Gary. "I got in," he said.

Kyla beamed. "To the Gesundheit Institute?"

"Yeah. All I got to do is make the patients laugh. And my girlfriend's coming out in a month on her way to Hawaii. She got this great internship doing dolphin work."

Hog's master came in with his plate of charred bird flesh and sat down near Shari to eat. Hog fell down onto his stomach in the middle of the room and farted.

"They go out in this boat," Gary said, "and they like play drums and chant until the dolphins come. They like get in the water with them. Apparently it totally works every time."

I asked where he was from. Kyla glared at me: don't start.

Thirty-one

A white guy with dreads down his back had just finished his nondairy lasagne and was having a little vegan cheesecake when I finally got a new sole onto a customer's favorite pair of UFO climbing slippers. Most of the adhesive had bonded pretty well, at least well enough to keep the sole from falling off by itself, so I stepped out onto the sales floor to put them up at the front desk. On my way back, a tall gray-haired woman in a yellow cotton dress smiled and asked if I worked there.

"I need a few things," she said. "I'm going to Nepal, and it's going to be very cold."

She took a folded piece of paper out of her suede purse and began to read: two sets of Everest Polarplus bibs ($125 ea.), two Everest Polarplus sweaters ($125 ea.), two sets of Everest 3-Layer Gore-Tex bibs ($275 ea.), two Everest Down Gore-Tex parkas ($399 ea.), two Everest Gore-Tex-shelled down sleeping bags rated to twenty degrees below zero ($629 ea.) and two pairs of Lowa Denali plastic mountaineering boots ($429 ea.). Total: @$4,000

"Why two?" I asked.

"For my guide," she said. "It's a vision quest trip I've arranged with this master in India who's just wonderful. We're going to climb a sacred mountain."

"You know," I said, "you can get most of this stuff used."

"Well," she said, "because of his spirituality, he can't use things that have been inhabited by others. And also, he specified Everest."

Thirty-two

Kyla played with Naomi's baby, Nora, on the plank floor of their living room, holding her arms up to help her walk. She told me with delight that she'd even given Nora her own dry nipple recently. Naomi, who was making us all a pot of spaghetti, seemed to love the thought of her little girl being so connected to a wise and sweet woman like her old friend Kyla. Kyla looked sideways at me as she bent down and said she wasn't at all sure she could wait the two-year minimum I'd put on having one ourselves. Right before us, she insisted, as Nora suddenly began to shriek in her tiny voice, was an example of how easy it could be—I didn't have to have a real job. Naomi and Christopher got along fine, rented a cheap house on the farm and lived within their means.

And what a house—no pavement anywhere for that little girl to skin her knees on, just a little blue bungalow in an overgrown meadow at the base of a wooded hillside. A big, rambling old oak tree in front of the porch shaded their beds of mint and basil and a string hammock hung in its branches. When it became clear that Kyla wouldn't be able to stop Nora's screaming, Naomi put on the pasta and came to get her. Christopher, tan and wiry in white chi pants and a turquoise tank top, packed a bowl of homegrown in a pipe baked out of chocolate-chip cookie dough. As he pressed in a purple-haired bud with his thumb, he talked about the big farm he'd just bought near Gardenville in Oregon. His dark, vein-covered hands put the pipe to his lips and he winked at the breast-feeding oblivious Nora as he inhaled.

Petite as she was, Naomi had large, pale, freckled breasts and they were stretched full with milk in her black cotton blouse. The baby nursed quietly—like her, it had curly, inky-black hair. The property in Oregon, Chris said, passing the pipe to Kyla, had great river frontage and a house lots of people could live in. And although the river used to be full of selenium, the authorities say they've cleaned it all up. Going to start with corn and hay and then get into some hormone-free livestock. Maybe an apple orchard. Get a real community going of like-minded folks. I could smell the garlic and oregano in Naomi's thick red sauce bubbling in the kitchen.

I was drinking a Bison Stout on a foam pad on the floor, and when Christopher stopped talking to take another hit, Kyla handed me a framed color photograph from Nora's birth. She leaned against me as I looked—Christopher and Naomi were sitting together in a white bathtub on an overgrown lawn of dead grass; while Chris looked frantic at being a bystander, Naomi appeared oblivious to his presence. I noticed there were no doctors, no nurses.

"Just midwives," Naomi said. She'd been teaching the old ways to the goodwives of the county: "They were the victims of the first witch-hunts." Nora stopped sucking and Naomi began to bounce her gently. "Yeah," she continued, "in the Middle Ages. Because they threatened the whole male medical structure."

Chris had made monthly plaster casts of Naomi's abdomen during the pregnancy—belly masks—and painted them with trees and streams, images of flowing life. Now the masks hung on the wall of their living room. The placenta was buried under the rosemary patch right outside, Naomi said, and they'd planned to have a placenta-eating ceremony but everyone they knew was vegetarian.

"I've done some rock climbing," Chris said, looking over to me. He nodded and closed his eyes as he held in a hit, then exhaled. "Never with ropes though. Too much technology. I'm more into just me and the rock." He picked up the plastic baggie of homegrown again and fished around for another bud. "I scrambled up a lot of peaks in the Trinity Alps last summer," he said, still fiddling with the bag, "some really steep stuff, too. Heights don't scare me that much, I'm just not into the whole technical trip. You miss out on all the plants and birds and get all wrapped up in conquering. Conquering's not what it's about in nature."

Naomi passed Nora to Kyla then buttoned her shirt. She checked the pasta, then came and sat on a pillow and silently watched her husband talk about a connection in Venezuela he had for varieties of vegetables that had been suppressed in the U.S. by big agribusiness. Naomi looked out the window toward the hammock in the oak tree, hugged her stomach with her twiggy little arms, and rocked gently back and forth. Kyla leaned forward just slightly as Chris talked, little Nora pulling all the while at her hair.

As we walked back to Kyla's tent after dinner, stumbling on roots in the dense forest darkness, Kyla told me how she was really thinking about going along with them to Oregon.

"Could you maybe live like that?" she asked. I said it sounded all right, but confessed I'd always thought of farming as serious labor for negligible gain. But sure, I'd live in the country. Especially with her. She bit my finger and growled without conviction.

The next morning we picked up Danishes and bad coffee at a roadside bakery and drove up to the Interdependence Festival in Salinas. On a baseball field in the summer heat a band played raunchy rock-and-roll while booths sold jewelry, crystals, massages, aural photographs, spirulina drinks, flower essences, rainsticks and organic pork sausage. For a hundred dollars each a hair-sprayed older woman in a pink leisure suit painted portraits. In the wooden subject chair sat a younger woman, strong jawed with small, close-together eyes, whose violet terry-cloth blouse had been reinterpreted as the cloak of the warrior, rider of night winds. Her valley-girl feathered hair had begun to flow into the head of an eagle and on her beady iris a tall, dark woman led a band of black-haired people in animal skins across an arctic waste.

We had apples and a baguette under a tree while Kyla tried to tell me about a class she'd just taken in Shamanism and witchcraft, another side to nature. I always saw the macro, she explained, the glacial valleys and tectonic uplift, the exfoliation domes and prehistoric oceans. And she was right. She would instead point me to the ground and say, "See, mugwort. Taste it. And this one's crimson columbine, you can see its ovaries." That afternoon, she explained only half-ironically that she was of the meadows and forests, I of the mountains and sea; she of earth and air, I of fire and water.

Thirty-three

Downpour on the high desert. Nick and I walked up out of the gorge with our parkas in our packs because the water coming down was as warm as the air rising up. When we reached the truck the rain stopped around us, but in the mountains up out of Bishop we could still see sheets of it dropping out of the clouds. The high country to the north remained dark and obscured by the storm as we drove toward the hot springs. At Crowley Lake General Store, we filled our plastic water jugs and bought tortilla chips and Mexican beer. Then we bounced the truck back the jeep track to a small spring in wide-open range.

Tired and blissful, I stripped in the evening zephyr, watched waves roll across miles of grass, and eased myself into the little rectangular concrete tub. One-hundred twelve-degree water was almost too hot to take and I lay still, the slightest movement burning. As sulfur found its way into every cut and scratch and lithium floated up with the steam, I watched the sun change phases and spectra, light up different strata of clouds, pick out mountainsides and steep faces for momentary red or orange glow, and then sink into twenty or thirty minutes of easing the sky from crimson haze to clear starlight. I could see the sharp, black fingers of the Minarets again up along bulky Mount Ritter and Banner Peak.

I floated with only eyes and nose in the air so my own breathing became a wind, my heartbeat an echo. After inhaling lithium for almost an hour, I stood up to dry off in the breeze; the heat left my body warm even in the cold air, so I stood dripping in the grass and tried to take in the face of Mount Morrison—its broad arching buttresses and deep gullies. An entire storm system moved down a weather corridor against the mountains to the east; rainbows followed and the whole fabric of a cloud split and poured down on the sunlit grazing cattle below. Tire tracks ran in circles through a muddy salt flat at the base of a meadow beside us. Three cows crowded around a sink pond a quarter mile away.

With a few too-spicy quesadillas we drank the beers and watched the storms clear, lost track of time breathing that wide-open air and drinking out in so much stillness. Once the sun had been down awhile and the color had left the sky, the moon lit up Morrison through the clouds as if by a flashlight, so singular was its aim. I was just thinking how much Kyla would love this place, when a pickup parked up the grade from us; a dark figure wearing a head-lamp came down to the muddy source pool that fed our little tub. He leaned over it and searched through its water, then turned and walked over the grass to us.

"Howdy fellas," he said, "how's it?" He leaned over and dipped a thermometer into the tub. "One twelve? That's not too bad. Wow. Dudes. Multiple-source adjustable cold-tap, yeah, this is all new. That wasn't here last time I was here, last time it was one twenty. Way too hot. So what are you all doing over here?"

Sitting on the tailgate we talked to this silhouette about the Gorge, about maybe going up to Tuolumne Meadows for a few days. He talked about Yosemite, where he was from, and made us promise to visit a hot spring somewhere near Strawberry, Nevada. He rambled about being a struggling folk artist and about his day job doing floors in Yosemite Valley for the Curry Company; I looked at the line between the black of the mountains to the east and the much lighter open cobalt of the sky. Nick told him about Wilbur Hot Springs up near Clear Lake, a sort of spa and artist's community where Nick thought the guy'd really fit in. He asked what the guy's medium was, and then had to explain that he just meant what kind of art does he do.

"Um . . . Beads?" the guy said, the interrogative uplift a Deadhead mannerism signifying sweetness.

"Like what?" Nick asked.

"Um . . . I do the geos? I've done the two? the four? the six and the eight? They're three-dimensional? and they're all beads and string?" Another dark figure—a friend of the first—appeared and sat down in the grass with a twelve-pack. The first asked if we'd ever heard the story of the spring.

"No?" he said, amazed. "This tub's got a little history." As he got comfortable in the grass, I got ready for great local lore, a far-western inside scoop.

"You see," he said, "this rancher's teenage daughter came out here all by herself like an idiot on a summer night and was sitting in the tub with no clothes on and she was really, really good-looking and she was having a beer listening to the radio of her daddy's bright red pickup when a bunch of drunk cowboys from out of Bridgeport showed up. Apparently she didn't leave real quick like she should've and next thing she knew she was getting gang-banged on the salt flat by all these crazy motherfuckers on their night off." He chuckled, enjoying his voice. "Yeah, so her old man got all pissed and dynamited the little shack that used to be over the tub here. That's why it's such a broken-down little tub. It used to have, you know, like a little house over it like the tub up out of Markleeville." He chuckled again and looked up at the moon.

His friend climbed into the back of their truck and passed out, never having set foot in the water. As I dozed off in the back of my truck, the historian worked his way back and forth between the source pool and the tub, checking temperatures, moving pipes, fiddling with rocks.

When Nick and I awoke the other two were asleep, their thin blankets soaked with dew. We closed up the truck to head for the Meadows. A fog bank engulfed Crowley Lake in the pre-dawn cold, filling this big valley between ranges with a lone cloud. Plumes of steam from other springs rose up from the plain like columns around a prayer ground.

Thirty-four

Well after dark, from the pay phone at the Yosemite Valley gas station, I called Kyla, told her I was down off the rocks and coming to see her. A spring storm hammered the dark empty highway with sleet; drops ran down the glass of the phone booth and formed a puddle around my feet.

"I was in the garden today," she said, "and we were talking about cutting things back and taking clippings. We were talking about making it an exchange, you know, giving some of your menstrual blood or some of your hair to the plant when you take part of it to use."

One of the instructors had laughed at her.

"We get one of you every year," he'd said. "There's always somebody who won't cut or kill anything."

"I just feel so bad," she said to me on the phone, pleading, "about all those little lives. Christopher's been spending a lot of time with me trying to work on death consciousness."

As Nick drove the truck under El Capitan I rolled down my window and shoved my head out into the downpour. High up on the Nose, I could just make out two head-lamps below the summit overhangs, bobbing around, blinking in and out of the storm.

Thirty-five

Walking up the dirt road from the farm parking lot, Kyla pointed out tall green stalks with hard balls on top—opium poppies that grew wild along the broccoli fields, surrounded the group house, and bled between the basketball court and the campground. A knife slit in their bulb would let the black opium sap out, and if dried, they were beautiful to hang around a room. In a bed beside the little fenced-off culinary and medicinal herb garden were California poppies: so different from the alien green spheres, they were a swath of richest orange fanning open in the late morning warmth. Folded closed for the cool night they'd been smaller, tighter. With the sunlight they spread out and laid their petals to flutter with the breeze. Behind the California poppies an Indian diva done in bronze sat in the weeds.

I was still stiff from the drive as Kyla took me by the hand through patches of fragrant rosemary, garlic, thyme, dill, oregano—a soft leafy little green herb, very sweet. Mugwort, Saint-John's-wort, dandelion, burdock—beautiful and healthy, they grew in clustered beds with quartz crystals in the soil. The greens tinted and shaded one another—pale green, bright green, the gray-green of sage, the rich darkness of rosemary. I kissed Kyla's soiled fingers and she gently pulled them away.

"Rub a leaf between your finger and thumb, like this." She smelled, and rolled her eyes. She bent down to tighten her sandals and watched expectantly as I began pinching off leaves. Each time I rubbed, an essence came off on my rock-sore, calloused fingers; each time more complex as the layers remained and blended. Tiny brown bottles of clary sage and geranium essential oils—for deepening and uplifting respectively—came out of Kyla's blue fanny-pack and we smelled; she was dabbling in aromatherapy. The aromas were so powerful, the oils so dense, that they held on in my nose long after, filtered into every other smell I breathed and did, if I thought about it, uplift me a bit and perhaps even deepen me.

"Don't lie," Kyla said, smiling and shaking her head at me.

Where tall, dark redwood forest leaned over the low beds, she sat on a bench and scraped opium sap from the poppies into a dragon-shaped pipe made of tin—unrefined it was almost ineffectual, and while we smoked she smiled knowingly at her friend the sassafras; she'd worked in that garden every day for a few months and still couldn't bear to pick anything.

"Do you know I even hate killing mosquitos?" she asked. "Do you think that's crazy?"

Also in her fanny-pack was a pouch of angel cards, and without warning she asked me to choose one. I felt around in the little leather bag with my eyes closed, then picked out a card. The word "light" was drawn in calligraphy below a graphic of a burning candle. It actually struck me as appropriate.

"Well?" she asked. I could tell she wanted a real answer, and I had this terrible, nervous impulse to giggle.

"Well," I said, managing to keep straight, "I've always thought of myself as a creature of light."

"Really?"

"Really. That's the truth." And it was.

She played with the beads on the end of a braid, suddenly saddened.

"Why didn't you ever tell me that before?"

Two cars pulled into the dirt lot below—showing up for the big Women's Weekend on the Farm. From their accounting and retail jobs, their law practices and medical rotations, they'd come to be the spiritual warriors they truly are.

"I've made an appointment with Beth," she said, "the woman who teaches the spirituality of plants up here. That's her car." In the parking lot I could see Beth stepping out of a brown Celica. It was hard to believe, but she actually wore a gold velvet dress and Egyptian leather strap sandals clear up her calves. In all seriousness and self-confidence. I could even hear the brass bracelets jangling on her arms. Kyla said Beth did the usual star charts and past-life readings, prescribed herbs and even crystals. She also chain-smoked Marlboros and drank six cups of coffee a day. Her husband, a scarred veteran of two tours in Vietnam, drank a six-pack of Coke every day and handled the male energy side of things.

Kyla decided we should get some lunch before the class monopolized the group house, so she put away the pipe and angel cards, and we got up from the bench. As we left the garden, a pale woman with silver and jade Navajo earrings and a green polyester jumpsuit stopped us. She didn't mean to be rude, she said, but once things had really started, I, as least, was to stay out of the group house. "It's going to be heavy," she said, shaking her head and squinting at the forest. We heard chanting from inside: "Power of the earth, power of the earth, power of the earth." Beating on a drum in the ninety-degree blank white light of California's coastal range.

While Kyla went inside to get food, I stood around in the dust and tried to stretch out my cramped forearms. I overheard two of the weekenders, eating tuna sandwiches on the front porch, trying to figure out an herbal equivalent of testosterone. A third explained that it was a hormone, so it was something from your body and there couldn't really be an herb of it.

Thirty-six

Off to climb the huge sorcerer's tower of Clyde Minaret up in the backcountry, Aaron charged ahead, and all day I needed breaks. He'd been doing construction for a friend in Berkeley, trying to get enough dough to buy junkyard parts for his broken-down Bug. He'd just given up on getting the right exhaust manifold when I'd asked him to go climbing. We had absurdly heavy loads—rock gear, storm gear and the usual full pile of camping gear added up to around seventy pounds; a dusty, painful trudge above the headwaters of the San Joaquin where I'd backpacked with Kyla. At the river crossing, the water ran high and cold. Early spring mosquito clouds found us quickly—humming, biting, sucking, splatting. Rocks on the creek bottom made carrying the packs barefoot difficult and painful, but snow-melt ice-water was a happy shock. Still, odd not to be able to drink any of it; must have been wonderful to just dip in a tin cup and pour the water down your throat.

Clyde Minaret disappeared from view and a long, gentle waterfall—right where Kyla'd made me do a sun salutation—roared white down a hundred feet of slabs. The manzanita and sparse fir were now surrounded with grass and yellow monkey flower. An acre of forest hit by an avalanche lay newly upturned as if by a vast plow—tree roots in the air, pine needles still green, adult firs thrown about like foot soldiers. The rangers had already been through with chainsaws, and stumps lay on each side of the path, raw ends staring across at one another.

At higher elevation snow appeared and the unfamiliar surface slowed me down as my boots punched through weaker spots and slipped on ice patches; when we topped out at Minaret Lake, late in the day and wiped-out, I was dizzy and achy with altitude and dehydration. Clyde Minaret, a pointed, crooked spire surrounded by snowfields, started another thousand feet above. While we cooked miso and black beans I tried to control nausea at having gone straight from sea level to eleven thousand feet.

"Way up there," I said, by way of evasion, looking up at Clyde. Feeling very, very spooked by the alpine exposure of the thing. It was a big step away from the Owens River Gorge, and even from the warm, low altitude granite of El Cap's East Buttress.

"Yeah, pretty far up there." He sounded thrilled. "You want to do the Nose next?"

"What?"

"The Nose. You want to do it?"

I asked if we could just focus on the beast before us.

All night I lay staring at the roof of our tent, listening to the wind whip the tent's rain-fly and hoping we'd wake up to a downpour. Then we could just politely bow out for a day, lie around, acclimatize, have a look at the weather the following day. An injury up there would be a disaster, with almost no chance for rescue and I'd heard big, loose rocks could come down like cannon balls. I also wondered as Aaron snored away if the social irrelevance of climbing didn't define its pleasure after all.

I thought I'd slept for a moment when I found myself awake again, thinking about the night before and playing guitar on the porch of the farm's group house. An alluring scene that wouldn't last—Kyla sounded increasingly serious about going to Christopher's place in Oregon.

I still hadn't slept at four o'clock when the alarm went and Aaron woke up. We pulled on boots and crampons and started walking in the dark without eating or drinking. The previous day's sun cups had hardened and the crampons—which I had never before used—bit beautifully. We kicked our way around the lake in the cold, over bands of rock and across snowfields. The frozen water lay as a field of white symmetry among the crags, outlined by the light transluscent blue of its melting and freezing borders.

Shadows lay quiet beneath these cliffs—many of the walls here had no names and were never climbed. Not the object of much imagination, they didn't reach distinct summits, or weren't steep enough to merit the long approach; mind alone endows a wall with a quality of action and transformation. The eastern sky over Nevada reddened; pools of scarlet filled in the wells between peaks. White snow and black rock became again points in a spectrum as the pale blues of the frozen lake brightened. Aaron had moved far above me. He walked with his shoulders slumped, tall and bulky, axe dangling from a limp hand, head hanging, ponytail tucked into his red jacket—minimum of effort learned from mind-numbing alpine slogs. His gait was constant in even switchbacks. The guy amazed me. Relentless and unpredictable, he seemed to have nothing to say on this trip, no yarns. I panted and stopped. There was no sound in the morning beyond our crunching steps and breathing, the shuffle of nylon clothing.

Gold poured into the pools of red as distant desert atmospheres glowed into sight. Clyde's shattered triangular face lightened in the sun's discriminating first spread of light; the black wall began to shine yellow and soften. On the snowfield at my feet, in a hardened sun cup, lay a perfect orange butterfly. Spring had drifted too high; without daylight the little icy dish was a museum case of winter. Without wind to flutter its wings or reveal its death, the butterfly could have been waiting for the sun to rewarm its blood. Aaron found a swallow with its eyes open: it, too, lay still in a suncup without sun. Higher up, there were two more butterflies, each in a bowl of its own.

Aaron started leading up the wall as sunlight struck us. I sat on a small ledge at the border of snow and rock—no birds, no sound, just the gear clanking, Aaron breathing; nothing living up these couloirs. Very, very far above so many places, Aaron moved still farther above me. He climbed quietly, never complaining, never revealing stress. He seemed to find all of it easy and pleasant, entirely within his abilities.

The stone had a polished quality; its reds and ambers flowed into closed corners; broken edges might form deep, secure holds or useless slopers. The quiet demanded attention—no tour busses, no highway nearby, no other climbers having a ball on the next route over—without howling weather, climbing was almost noiseless. Whenever Aaron paused above, all was still. A beautiful solitude, but one that cast the enterprise in stark relief. Just doing something because it felt good. Clouds over the Clark range diffused the rising sun and the air remained cold, dry and windless. As I belayed from beneath a block the size of an economy car I could hear Aaron above. A small rock bounced next to me and then I watched it skip into the air over the snow. I followed its fall, but never heard it land.

I followed Aaron for hours over staircaselike blocks and into a long, broad dihedral—solid handjams, beautiful stemming, in the crack, out of it on good face holds, a full rope-length of exquisitely varied moves with good protection. Exhaustion from the hike and the night before, from dehydration and the altitude, never quite left me, and I found myself drifting off to sleep at belay ledges hundreds of feet into the sky. The snowfields far below gave the feeling of a static world occupied only by our meaningless and utterly fulfilling little quest.

Late in the day we finally reached the summit ridge; the view soared out to the broad black peaks of Mounts Ritter and Banner and over to Iceberg and Ediza Lakes—flat, snow-covered floors tucked into granite bowls. Farther out lay Thousand Islands Lake, not yet surrounded by the fish-

ermen's horse camps where in the summer guys get physically carried around the mountains to hassle fish.

Energy fading, I stepped over, slipped under and side-
stepped wild, sharp chunks of mountain as I looked for the
summit. Aaron finally got us there; deep, long gullies
dropped away—white triangles amid dry black ramparts.
The little plastic tube holding the summit register civilized
the place, even suggested safety. The promise of a needle-
point peak had been a ruse—it was just a couple of blocks
among many, a spot the surveyors had finally chosen for the
register. Low clouds stretched in and rubble fell away in all
directions—brown rock piled on top of more rock. To the
west, arid cirques, ridges and high bowls locked together
over long, deep valleys of ferns, wildflowers, and meadows—spring living just below winter, pushing up.

And that was that. A hike, a sleep, an approach, a
climb, a summit. A story. A ceremony of goals clean and
personal, unmitigated by compromise. A little, repeated
tale about ourselves that we told each time we picked a new
summit and sought it out. And always just after the exuber-
ance of the summit came a faint disappointment that the
real pleasure, the process, the living with order, purpose
and energy in a magnificent place, was over.

After two hours of short, hard steps down through
loose blocks and little snow patches, we began to rappel—
hanging free on the rope, rotating with its twists past huge,
dark, wet chunks of stone; north-facing, shaded alcoves
still coated with ice. Places unused and unseen, and nothing gained or lost by it. Ropes, slings, harnesses: small sys-

tems applied to the periphery of a massive, unstable form. So different from cragging where one participates in a set of belay anchors, rappel points and climbing routes etched all over the cliff and inscribed in books.

I touched down on snow. Aaron had kicked a platform for me on the slope. Suddenly too tired to concentrate, I started to walk while Aaron did all the work of coiling the ropes. I didn't even offer and he didn't complain. I had no sense of whether the snow would give beneath my weight or resist and let me slide. Steps were fairly easy to kick, but still I faced uphill, axe in deep, one foot at a time. Aaron caught up quickly, walking sideways, letting his steps slide and stop, glissading a little, moving fast.

Then my feet shot out from under me, I slammed down on my chest, and I rocketed toward a huge patch of blue ice. Below the ice were bands of cliffs. I pulled up the axe, sank the pick and stopped quickly. Aaron laughed and kept running.

The trudging and dehydration lasted for hours. At water running through a snow slope we sat for a while and drank, tried to pick out our tent down below. The sun, a smear of pale gray in darker clouds, faded gradually out. Night came on as we recrossed frozen inlets of Minaret Lake. I found myself walking with eyes closed, ankles wobbling, feet limp, nearly falling down as my boots slipped into sun-cups; pain I had sought and now drank happily. In the unspoken esthetic of such days, this one had been perfect—awake long before dawn, home well after dark; hard output all day, both hiking and climbing, and yet no epics, no disasters. A real summit of a real object, attained by the most direct of routes. I was thoroughly and profoundly tired, from mind to muscle to feet, and knew full well that was precisely what I'd wanted.

Finally, the tent. Getting pretty sleepy, I wondered if I'd be warm enough to snooze without getting into my sleeping bag. Far too much effort required. As I lay face down in the tent, pack still on, boots sticking out the door, Aaron said something.

"I was just wondering if you're still psyched to walk out tonight. We could probably make it to the base of the Nose tomorrow afternoon."

I couldn't even get it together to tell him what a joke that was.

Aaron stayed up by himself for a while and made miso soup, looked over a route map of the Nose that he'd started carrying around with him. The guy wanted walls. I heard him mutter something just before he drifted off about getting his Kiwi friend Peter to do the route with him.

In the morning we both heard a noise outside the tent. Aaron scrambled out of his sleeping bag and out into the sun, falling across dirty pots and wet boots. He cursed, then hurled a rock at a marmot. Three of the monstrously over-sized squirrels had ripped open our food bag where we'd stashed it in a bear-proof cleft in a boulder.

"Got to nail 'em," he said.

"Why's 'at?"

"Keep 'em wild. This is bullshit where they're so used to people. Of course you don't feed 'em, but you also gotta fuckin' nail 'em."

Gear was strewn everywhere in an absolutely slovenly display. Uncoiled yellow ropes spilled out of my black summit pack and lay across the trail, ice axes sat on the ground, our big backpacks were half-disemboweled with rock gear, water bottles and sunscreen. After an hour or so of sunshine, oblivion in the little patch of green grass, soreness and what granola the marmots hadn't finished, we packed slowly and set off—sore feet stumbling back down the trail, tension relieved. No goal ahead except a hamburger. Times like this—serious protein deficiency—separate the vegetarians from the posers.

Aaron practically ran ahead down out of winter and back through the phases of spring. Near the end, the trail was so pounded-out from horses' hooves we could've driven a bus most of the way home—a six-foot-wide sand track threaded its delicate way through the woods. Water from seasonal creeks washed still more of the trail away, leaving a broad, muddy mess. Soon, knees wobbling and feet swelling, we were in sight of the headwaters of the San Joaquin again and the deep green meadows and clear water—how I was lusting for water. The tin-cup-in-the-stream fantasy had become an all-consuming fixation, an absolute outrage. Letters to congressmen formed in my head—legislation requiring the surgical implantation of catalytic converters in the digestive tracts of all alpine horse and cattle stock. Then families appeared and a body-built group of muscular sports fans hiked past wearing survival knives and camo tank tops.

In the town of Mammoth Lakes we got enormous burgers—straight-up, guilt-laden red meat.

"Probably took four hundred pounds of grain that could have fed a thousand people just to make that one pound of beef," Aaron said, just as I was shoving the whole pile into my mouth. I held it for a moment and looked up, jaw open. "Yup," he said, "probably straight from Brazilian ex–rain forest."

I told him the late, brilliant Edward Abbey hated cows so much for all the damage they do to land that he ate all the hamburgers he could—"Only good cow's a dead cow." We smoked a bowl in the supermarket parking lot before trying to face the universe of packaged food options. Stocked-up and laughed-out we headed for the springs.

Soaking at last, the sun setting yet again, I watched the cattle move in on the source pool ten yards away. A few at first, then fifteen snorting, slobbering cows were all climbing into the warm water that bubbled through tubing down to us. A bull of obscene muscle mass looked our way occasionally, his place undisputed. A restless calf bucked and bolted out to the brackish salt swamp down the wash.

Thirty-seven

Viewed from an amphitheater of roses set into a wooded Berkeley hillside, the sky out over the sharp blue Pacific appeared deep orange; the black silhouettes of Mount Tamalpais and the Golden Gate Bridge were etched just like I'd remembered them across the sunset and a warm breeze fell down off the hills. On the bike ride up, Kyla had coughed in the exhaust of a bus, but now she held a yellow rose bud to her nose and smiled.

"Dan," she said, when I asked how the Women's Weekend had gone, "it was the most incredible thing that ever happened to me. You've got to come back down. I swear you'd love it if you spent more time. It's so much like what you used to do with your family." Chris had begun buying supplies for the big move; a few more people had signed on to join the community and I'd told Kyla I wasn't too interested. Maybe I'd have to look into guiding climbing, or working in a national forest. I also hadn't seen her in a couple of weeks. She looked healthy and radiant and had cut, washed and combed her blond mop; she'd even taken the last few braids and dreads out.

An oil tanker moved in under the Golden Gate Bridge, heading for the Port of Richmond in the northern part of the Bay. I'd been wrecking shoes again at the mountain shop, trying to figure out how to make the new soles stay on longer than a few hours. Aaron had come by that afternoon wanting to return to the backcountry. He had a route in mind up on Bear Creek Spire and I'd told him I'd go.

Kyla was playing with her hair as two middle-aged women in khakis and running shoes walked down into the rose gardens. Kyla's fingers looked stronger and had dirt worked deeper into their callouses. When I told her I couldn't come down until after the climb, she went on talking about the weekend. "I took an herbal wedding class," she told me. "We made like garlands and looked at herbs magically for what you want to put in the bouquet." She was still wearing a crown of flowers she'd made; I could smell the jasmine.

"Pretty different trajectory for you, huh?"

"Than what?"

"Than the aggro Yosemite Festival scene?" I was thinking of the lesbian gathering that had scared her off a while back, how different these versions of the women's scene were.

"No." She looked at me for a while, wondering what the hell I'd meant, then went on: "Anyway, I also took a class on Chinese barefoot doctor stuff, like cupping, where you suction an area of the skin under a water glass and it gets really grotesque. From the color you can tell what's wrong." A sailboat had passed Alcatraz and was slipping by the oil tanker to leave the Golden Gate. Odd to be departing the bay at this hour.

"And at night the drum circle ended in a wild witch thing with everyone dancing around naked to drums under a full moon, throwing their bodies everywhere." She was thrilled by the thought. "Just like woman-passionate nakedness, dancing in circles and chains and spinning with fat people and skinny people and old people, little crazy girls and families of three generations of women. I know it sounds like a cliché," she said, looking me in the eye, "but it was the real thing and like you had to just decide you were going to be there and not trip on what it was trying to be. I really think I love that stuff. It's like picking a way to live, you know." I nodded, thinking I did know.

Kyla held a new crystal Naomi had given her. "When everyone was tired we started putting ourselves out there, just saying, you know, whatever you want to say. Like I asked right at the beginning, 'I've always wanted this, and I've always been afraid to ask, but will everyone sing my name?' And so everyone started singing 'Kyyylaaaa!'"

"You've always wanted that?"

She thought about it for a moment, then decided that yes, she had. "And one woman said, 'An hour ago I found out my beautiful little sister was raped in New York and could we all call out to her?' So right there fifty California women held hands around the fire and chanted this poor New York girl's name all the way across the country in the middle of the night."

We rode our bikes back down Euclid Avenue and across campus in the twilight. On College Avenue we stopped to rent a movie. Gorging on free popcorn, we argued: I voted for one about a man alone in Alaska studying wolves; Kyla yawned and lobbied for a macabre white trash romance on the seedy byways of the South. We settled on an early Woody Allen and rode home through crosstown traffic.

Thirty-eight

Aaron turned twenty-one and wanted to get in a fight.

"Go into a bar somewhere and get in a fight. Maybe get beaten up. Yeah, I want to get beaten up. Not too bad though."

He settled for just trying to get carded. At the log cabin Rock Creek Lodge up out of Tom's Place, California, Aaron put on a clean T-shirt, shaved, tucked his ponytail into a baseball cap, walked in to buy beer and wine with a handful of change and tried to sound embarrassed and nervous, and for the first time in his life was not asked to prove his age. We drank the six-pack of Sierra Nevada Pale Ale directly out in front—Aaron was holding out for Drinking in Public. No luck. They did, however, have homemade chocolate-chip cookies five for a buck.

Up at the lake in an asphalt lot among evergreens, RVs were everywhere, jeeps in tow. A cold, hard wind came off the mountains and chilled the sunless canyon where we'd parked. We turned the truck into the wind and cooked in back under the camper shell—refried black beans, whole wheat tortillas, scallions, tomatoes and salsa.

Aaron hit the magnum of Barefoot cabernet while I

was still on my last burrito.

"Amanda," he said, looking out at the wind-streaked lake. "Got to find her." He drank again from the wine, then turned the bottle over to read its label.

"Who's 'at?"

"Girl I met in Alaska." He closed an eye and looked with the other down inside the bottle.

"Alaskan?"

"Nah. She's from Seattle. Goes to school up there."

"Really dig her?"

"Yeah. Pretty outrageous. I met at her at Denali base-camp. Spent a couple weeks digging the hell out of each other in the mountains." He passed me the bottle and I took a drink before setting up our little stove. "She's like almost perfect. Totally hot looking, really smart. Solid ice and rock climber. Leads like 5.10. Dancer. Man, I drove all the way to Seattle a few months ago, supposedly going to make money for school. Totally planning to blow it off and cruise back to Alaska with her. Take like a year and just go nuts, you know, climb Denali, hang out on the Talkeetna Glacier with this knockout, maybe work the fishing boats up there and make a fortune so we could head for Indonesia. Whole bit."

I finally got the stove going and its jet roar echoed in the hollow, metallic space of my camper shell. Aaron pulled a Friend out of a milk crate. He sat there bundled up in Levis, running shoes, black pile jacket and red Gore-Tex shell, altogether absorbed in the Friend and holding its axle up close to his eyes.

"So?" I demanded.

"Her?"

"Yeah."

"Blazed all night in the bug, all day too. Not even eating. Straight through Oregon, through all those outrageous northern forests. Got to Seattle thinking it'd be just like Alaska. I roll up and she's right there on the street in front of her folks' really nice brick house and she was just like, 'Oh, hi Aaron.' Like I was an irritating neighbor. I didn't even stay the night.

"I was so freaked out, I got on the highway and drove north for about six hours crying and running red lights in tiny Canadian towns before I decided to head home. Never stopping. Not till I ran out of gas. I felt really sad. This trucker helped me out with the gas, though."

In the morning we sorted gear in an arc around the truck. A white-haired, bent-backed old park ranger, probably in his seventies, came strolling into the parking lot chatting with some day hikers. He came over to talk to us and I saw "wilderness permit" in his eyes, something we didn't have and weren't in the mood to get. I knew I had to head him off at the pass, ask him something distracting. Ask him if he knew how much snow was up at Dade Lake.

"Frozen solid," he said. "You prepared for snow camping?"

I asked if he knew of ice or snow up on the face of Bear Creek Spire.

"Son," he said, "how many axes you got? You got crampons?"

He told us how he'd been a ranger up here fifty-six years and they'd finally let him name something—a big peak up north and east of Bear Creek Spire. The big chance to leave his mark.

"Well," he said, "the lakes at the base of it are called Treasure Lakes, so I called it Treasure Mountain."

The trail turned out to be an old road—mushy and muddy, pounded and stinking with stagnant puddles in hoof holes. At a low lake a quarter-mile out a man in a meadow appeared to be proposing to his beloved. She sat on a log with her knees in her arms as he kneeled before her. The mosquitos were utterly barbaric as we passed.

We marched up along a series of lakes where the trail had been blasted out of rock walls; there must have been commercial fishing camps there once, or mines. Off north were huge sheer walls of granite that probably had never been climbed—they didn't hit any particular summit and looked hard to get to. Bear Creek Spire, viewed from the approach, rose as a curving ribbon of white stone to a pointed peak; viewed from other angles, it was a rubble pile, but a climber demands only one inspiring facade.

We set up the tent at three o'clock out on an island in the middle of frozen Dade Lake at eleven thousand feet. Behind white boulders amidst broad snowfields, big bowls of snow rising up to the mountain above, we lay still all afternoon. On our backs. Not even reading. Although it was very cold, the sun penetrated and I felt a sneaking desire to hide. I covered my head with a T-shirt and even hid my hands. So white and clear, unfettered, unfiltered, the sun burned without heat.

"She's out in the Cascades doing bear work," Aaron said, lying nearby, also hiding, "some kind of research on

what they eat." The Spire was there all day for us to con-
template, to pick out a route. "Intense, huh? Girl who can
just vanish into the woods like that?"

There were no mice, no birds, no marmots. Aaron
rolled over to inch into a sliver of shade. Insulated from the
cold air by my clothes, I felt solar heat now. Exposed skin
burned quickly.

"I got to give it another shot with her," he said. "But
they'll never tell me where she is."

More out of boredom than hunger, I started making
dinner. I cut the onions slowly and set them aside. Then the
cheese. The warmth had slowed things down while wind
kept the air dry and brittle. Breathing parched my nostrils
and throat and made a windy sound through the T-shirt on
my head.

"It was amazing," Aaron said, looking a little sad. "I've
never connected with anybody at every level, emotionally
and physically. She's a great climber, really into red meat,
really great sex like all over these mountains. Pretty fear-
less. Likes to drive way too fast. I'm not positive, but I think
I was pretty much in love with her. Think I'll just head out
to the Cascades and look around. Bound to find her. Maybe
get her to bail and take off for a year and drive around."

"Think it'll be different from last time, huh?"

"Has to be."

"She'll just bail?"

"I gotta do something stupid to make her."

I opened a can of organic vegetarian refrieds and shov-
eled them into our pot. Aaron rolled over to watch me cook.
I made us each an overflowing burrito, then lay quietly for a

while before making another. We'd rationed food for the
following night as well, but there was little else to do
besides eat it all. More burritos, then an afternoon nap.
Emptying out in the warmth and silence of this small
winter.

After a long sleep we made miso. It still wasn't dark,
but the sun had moved behind a ridge and the wind had
become colder. Still, we sat by the boulders and looked up
at the climb. Like Clyde, it had that quality of the perfect
task: a real summit, a clean, direct line. Sitting below in anticipation was the perfect kind of peace: behold your chosen task. The route also looked reasonably easy, although
there was a steep section. The Sierra Club guide was, as
always, remarkably useless: "Climb the prominent arête."

We finished the miso and began brewing chamomile
tea. The light began to change higher up on the ridgelines,
creating distinct shadows and fields of bronze. Aaron was
stuffing our hardware into his summit pack when he asked
if I'd thought any more about the Nose. He still had the little El Cap route map in his pocket.

"A little," I responded, spooked at just talking about it.
There wasn't a climb anywhere I wanted more, but the idea
of going up there before I was good and ready seemed stupid. "You really think we can pull it?"

"No problem. It's just rock."

"Shouldn't we do Half Dome first?"

"No way."

At four in the morning, we started slogging up to Bear
Creek Spire. Far off east I watched the sun first warm the
deserts, then slip across into the fertile valleys below the

Sierra. Exhausted, panting and nauseous, I stopped in my tracks every few hundred feet to watch Aaron. As we got up into the last snowfield beneath the spire, the Rock Creek drainage out to Long Valley, began to warm and shine. Lakes reflected the dawn up into our sheltered cirque like tiny flecks of mica at the bottom of a creek.

The rock was solid and exquisite—good protection and fun climbing. Moving quickly, pulling hard on solid holds, we simulclimbed the entire route, running upward on all fours. Panting at thirteen thousand feet, we were loving the oxygen debt and yelling and laughing at each other.

On top we had lunch by the register—all of it more Dionysian than Odyssean. Photocopies inside showed the original entries from Norman Clyde and then later ones from David Brower and other Sierra Clubbers, huge crews of grinning, healthy men and women in knickers. The present register went back only about seven years, not long enough to find my parents' entry. It seemed like once a year, though, the name of my friend Mark Long was in there. It got to be comical—Mark Long, July 1985, A great day for climbing, beautiful weather; Mark Long, March 1986, Another beautiful day for skiing and climbing! Mark Long, April 1987, A lovely day for climbing and skiing! I remembered a guy I met in Mammoth once saying, "Oh yeah, Mark Long, I know that name. It seems like every time I ski a peak he's been up there seven times before me with his dog."

Coming down we rappelled about a hundred feet off the back of the spire, then followed talus to snowfields. The enormous quiet planes of space were a ball to run through.

Exquisite relief, soaring along. Once we got to the top of
the steep snowfields that dropped back to our camp—
about two thousand vertical feet—Aaron just pointed his
boots downhill and started sliding. I couldn't quite get it
together to believe I wouldn't tumble and go rocketing out
of control into a boulder somewhere. Impatient, Aaron
finally yelled up at me to just sit on my butt. Perfect. With
my axe behind me as a rudder I ripped past him, bounced
off suncups, slipped through a few clumps of rock and
then down, down, down toward the lake. Nothing to do
but smile and scream.

Back at Rock Creek Lodge we showered before sitting
down to beers, burgers and pie. A huge American couple
next to us finished salads and ordered bowls of chili, then
more chili. Then grilled cheese sandwiches. Then more
grilled cheese sandwiches. Then he mumbled something
about needing to stand up. He waddled off to a backcountry topo map and looked it over. His woman friend ordered
them each a piece of lemon pie. The slices were comical—
five inches high—two or three bites just to get down
through them. They were talking about the Grand Canyon,
maybe driving up to Reno. The lemon pie was so good, and
so clearly made on the spot, that they decided to try the
mud pie. Two slices. As the man finished his off, he winked
at the waitress, smiled, and said, "Do you have somewhere I
can give birth?"

Thirty-nine

After sweating together all night in the mothers-with-babies section at a Dead show, Kyla and I drove for hours across the Central Valley and up into the coastal hills; back to the farm and her tent, back to her open-air bed in the redwood forest. Stepping out of the Ghia we both felt things happening; quiet drumming in the darkness of the garden, low chanting in the lightless group house. A candle protected by a hand lit the faces of three women wrapped in Guatemalan blankets. They stood on the dirt path before us, light from the little flame picking out a cheekbone here, the tip of a nose there, casting still blacker shadows into the well of an eye.

"A man!" one whispered.

Croning. Beth's hysterectomy had brought on early menopause and the women of the countryside were there to celebrate. "These rituals all kind of got lost a long time ago," Kyla said softly in my ear, pulling me away from the house, "so some women want to bring them back."

Near where the path to her tent led up the hillside, just as we were about to turn into the forest and toward bed,

Kyla looked back. A candle now burned somewhere in the kitchen and the chanting had grown louder. "I totally buy it," Kyla whispered as we stood on the dirt road. "I hate how in America we make old people seem useless, especially old women, because they don't make money and aren't sexy. But in olden times they used to be the wise women." She had turned now to watch dark figures file into the garden. I could smell sweat and incense in her hair. I was so exhausted from dancing and driving that I was dying to go to bed; after a week in the truck with Aaron, I wanted to curl up with Kyla.

"Crone's a pretty sacred stage in a woman's life," Kyla offered, still watching, "when what she gives her community is spiritual power. I can totally think of that in modern life. Look, there's Naomi with Nora on her back." Kyla spoke of croning as if she knew she couldn't convince me but demanded my respect. Only fair, really, and I tried to think of a universal principle or a social utility behind the ritual that would let me suspend doubt. It wasn't hard to do, and for once I felt honest about admiring the scene. She knew how hokey this stuff could sound to the skeptic, but she also knew the cost of life without the sacred was too high for her.

"I should probably go too," she insisted. "Beth might be bummed if I don't."

Beth of the golden velvet mini-dress, anklets and eye-shadow; one of wisdom's many forms. Kyla squeezed my hand and walked away. I saw her step into the garden, then stop just outside the now wide circle of women standing among the garden rows. She put her hands in her jeans pockets and looked back at me for a moment; I couldn't see her face in the darkness. Then she moved into the crowd.

I shivered in my stinking synthetic long underwear and leaned against an oak tree to wait. A flame lept up in the middle of the circle and Naomi, in her timorous, church choir voice, called out "Anu," the name of the Crone. She exhorted the gathering to embrace the power they all possessed of life and birth. To the fire, she announced, she had added a chaste tree branch, invoking the Goddess Ceres. Beneath the crescent moon they cried together in what sounded to me like forced enthusiasm mixed with practiced primal scream; but that's how I wanted it to sound.

Her baby in a sling on her back, Naomi read briefly from the Book of the Dead as they all held hands around a medicine wheel. I wondered where Christopher was, if maybe he was out drinking with the guys. Then Beth came to the fore. "Back during the great matriarchies," she began, "in ancient times . . . " All before her nodded in understanding: "Yes . . . back then."

I went on up the path by myself, barely able to see the poison oak patches; I pulled up on the branches of little bay trees and tried not to slide out of my sandals. A limb caught at my eye and I blinked just in time. Back at the little wooden platform I took off my clothes outside the netting, then quickly fell asleep inside. Sometime later I awoke and found Kyla sleeping beside me, still wearing her sweater and jeans.

Forty

A week later, I woke up between dirty sheets on my futon in Berkeley, fresh out of an embarrassing dream about Kyla and already thinking about the Nose. Aaron had talked me into it, but I still didn't have his conviction in my immortality. And for the past few months, every time I'd seen so much as a photograph of the Captain I'd gotten Pavlovian sweaty palms and chest constrictions. Somehow I'd become convinced that I had to do it, that otherwise I'd never be satisfied with my life. It was just so big and absolute. And to have done it . . . Dad wanted me to do Half Dome first, but Aaron was my only potential big wall partner and he wanted the big stone. Now. It seemed like he had an allergy to proper preparation, like it was a sign of weakness.

The apartment where I lay thinking about it was still more Kyla's than mine, although she was barely there anymore. A large studio with high ceilings, white plaster walls and hardwood floors, the whole place looked over Berkeley's tree-filled Elmwood district and out at the Golden Gate; Mount Tam to the north and the Transamerica Pyramid directly west. Around the molding were dried flowers in beautiful bouquets: roses, daisies, opium poppies, wysteria, lavender, wheat.

Two leafy green ficus trees, three phallic cacti, a bromeliad—so many of Kyla's plants crowded every corner of the room that between all that oxygen and the sweet scent of flowers, nothing short of a home waterfall could have improved the air quality. Whenever I reached for salt or pepper my hand still had to avoid the damiana, golden seal and burdock root; eyedroppers of herbal tinctures still surrounded my shaving cream in the bathroom cabinet. Looking for a clean razor I knocked a bottle of Saint-John's-wort out of the medicine cabinet. It shattered into little brown shards in the porcelain sink.

I walked out into the sunshine on College Avenue and got a cup of Kenyan and an orange-currant scone at Royal Coffee. At a green metal sidewalk table I distracted a friend from his Public Policy school applications. Neurotic and extroverted son of a UC Berkeley chemist, he'd decided early in life he wasn't cut out for science. He started telling me about creative financing for nonprofits when Tracy and Brynn showed up. They too got coffee and sat down. Tracy had just gotten a Julius Caesar haircut and wore a bronze cardigan with pale green jeans and Italian leather sandals. I told them all I was thinking about trying the Nose.

"Why?" asked the chemist's son. A great question. I could've given Hillary's answer—"because it was there"—and conversation would've moved briskly along, but I decided to be honest:

"I haven't the foggiest idea."

I broke off some scone to dip in the coffee and tried to think of a better answer. I almost mentioned the combination of El Cap's vastness and irrelevance, how it might just be big enough to be ontologically real, but decided to drop it. Tracy had recently been accepted to a graduate program in design, and while Brynn told the others about the courses he'd be taking, I got on my mountain bike and rode down to the mountain shop.

I'd finally figured out how to get a new sole onto a pair of shoes without changing their fit by more than a size, but the randing still had me stumped. Rands were the one-inch rubber strips wrapped around the base of climbing shoe uppers, and they had to be stretched on carefully; they defined much of the shoe's shape and if done improperly could radically alter it. I'd only done a few customer rands, and a pair of Tao boots had already come back with an outraged note. The guy not only wanted the shop to redo the work, but to pay damages for two lost toenails; apparently I'd shrunk his shoes into tension-loaded compression boxes.

I heated up his poor Taos and ripped all my miserable work back off, taking some of the remaining mid-sole with it; the faux-leather hulks were getting pretty torn down from all the abuse. Then I started trying to cut new rand patterns, thinking maybe that was the problem. I had this big black sheet of rubber out on my workbench and was carving into it with a hook-billed knife when Nick came in talking to the mountain bike freak. He wanted to know how the freak dealt with the environmental havoc he caused.

"Horses do way more damage," the freak responded, wearing the same purple visor, purple jersey, purple shorts and purple tights he wore every day. He leaned over to watch me spread ultra-toxic glue onto the rands. I suggested he take a deep breath.

"Yeah," Nick said, still wanting an answer, "but like, fully ripping around turns, watching little rabbits bolt into the bushes?" Nick had been hanging out in town, working at the shop a lot. Not climbing too much. He'd met a great new woman and his aggression level had tapered off significantly; he had, however, been talking about Half Dome a bit, how he wished I'd do it with him before rushing off to the Captain. His sudden ambition was suspicious.

"Look," the freak said, shaking his head, "before we start this conversation I should probably tell you, I'm an eco-fascist." He took off the visor for a moment to adjust the bun of long hair he kept rolled up behind its band. "Gotta keep my middle-class costume intact," he mumbled to himself, then continued. "Because these days it's like, hell, better put a tramway up to the top of Whitney, because otherwise we're discriminating against people in wheelchairs." He was leaning on our iron floor jack, pulling on his mustache as he talked. Nick had gotten another tidy haircut a week before and had taken to hiding it under baseball caps. That day he wore a navy blue one with the word "Icy" written on it. I put down the shoe to let it dry and started rummaging around in the stockroom for some of the big wall gear Aaron said we needed.

"Yeah," Nick said, "but hardcores like you break the trail, and the philistines follow. Before you know it there'll be an article in *Outside* magazine about 'Ten Great Mountain Bike Tours Across the Sierra, Complete with What Outfit You Should Wear.'"

A haul bag. I had to buy a real, white, Fish haul bag. The army duffel from the column had been retired to laundry duty.

"Bullshit," the Freak blurted, with a little mist for emphasis. "Sure everybody in Boulder, Santa Cruz, Berkeley and Eugene has a mountainbike. But most of them just want to wear their little tights and rip up an occasional meadow."

And another rope. Holy smokes, we needed another rope for the King Swing, the epic, horizontal sprint in the sky. My palms were, not surprisingly, damp.

"But dude," Nick said, "mountain biking is pretty raucous on the land."

"You know, the other day in Tilden Park these geriatric Sierra Clubbers were like, 'You're disturbing the animals! How can we get any solitude?' and I'm like, 'Hey! Have you ever kryptonited your neck to a tree to save it?! Well I have!'"

I couldn't believe what I'd heard.

"Did you really do that?" I yelled from a heap of Gore-Tex bibs. The freak yelled back that he had; I decided that gave him at least a little credibility. Neither Nick, Aaron, Kyla nor I was ever going to be able to make a claim like that.

Photocopy the route map. Make two copies on the shop Xerox machine, then laminate them in wrapping tape so they won't tear or fall apart if it rains. Jesus, the route looked long. Pitch after pitch after endless pitch, and none of it easy. Guys apparently got stuck up there for whole weeks sometimes. The failure rate for first-time parties was rumored to be nine out of ten.

"Tilden, too," the freak went on, "you know, I mean it's one thing if you're talking about a true wilderness area, but Tilden's a completely trashed multiuse area anyway. This is a complex topic, Nick. We could talk all day and still not get to the bottom of it."

And more thermals. And what about Gore-Tex. I'd heard that storms up there were so powerful that Gore-Tex was useless. You had to have absolutely waterproof, non-breathable, bombproof slickers. Water apparently could blow dead sideways and even straight up. Cracks could turn into little fire-hoses. And once you were wet, you stayed wet. Aaron thought he'd just bring a garbage bag. Figured if anything, it'd probably be too hot. Anyway, he figured, at some point you may as well stay home.

"I'm just wondering," Nick said, trying again, "if you personally feel any qualms about the damage."

"I don't cause any."

And gloves? Did I need gloves for multiple rappels in case we had to bail? How about a book on self-rescue techniques? Or a helmet? If Aaron (or I!) took a screamer and cracked something, neither of us would have any idea how to get ourselves down. I knew there were tricks, but didn't even know where to look to learn them. And it seemed kind of late. And my pulley for the haul bag—I had no idea if it was the right kind, or how the hell was the best way to haul.

Aaron and I were a great team, but man, we weren't super fast, and God, if you had thirty-two pitches to do and you were moving slowly . . .

"Ok, but as an eco-fascist, dude, shouldn't you be putting Mama Earth first? Like at least admit you play a part in the entropy."

"Nick," the freak said, smiling magnanimously, "it's just such a complex topic. I should give you some books to read."

The glue on the Taos and the new rands had dried and it was time to bond them: Nick heated up the shoe leather while I heated the rubber. Then he held the shoe in place; I began at the toe and stretched the rand back, pressing it down with my fingers as I moved toward the heel. In a moment the rand was attached. I threw the shoe onto the iron jack, grabbed a hammer, and started pounding on the rubber so the glue would hold.

"Dude," Nick said without looking at me, "I'm kind of serious about Half Dome." I wound up, swung hard right at the instep of the shoe, missed the rubber by a quarter of an inch, and ripped the whole side of the shoe open. Nick raised his eyebrows and took off his cap.

"Beauty."

The Cowboy Junkies tape started that song "Misguided Angel" and I dropped the hammer on the floor. The shoes were toast. No way around it. We'd have to give the bastard a new pair. The manager was going to love me. I tried to rethink the big picture: Design School, Public Policy, Shoe Repair. The Nose.

"Yeah," I said to Nick, "I'm stoked for the Dome too."

"I'm starting to think I need something big."

"No kidding. I just wish Aaron would wait."

Trip—the washer of car windows—appeared outside the grate by the workshop. I hadn't seen him in a while.

"Manager around?" he asked, shirt off, strong and lithe, "I'm um . . . is my friend with the long hair around?" I got the ski guru from the sales floor where he was reading a magazine. Trip had a framed charcoal of a nude, said he thought maybe he could do graphic arts work for us, could the guru just talk to the manager, see about his making signs? The guru took the drawing and went back into the store. Trip stood in the sun looking bigger and more toned than ever. I asked where he'd been lately, thought maybe it was a bad question.

"Just got out of Santa Rita," he said. Nick picked up the guidebook to Yosemite—the "resoling area only" copy—and flipped to the page about Half Dome. "Thirty-four years and never been in jail, but they finally got me. Just out there on the street cooling with my people and they get me for public drunkenness. Thirty days." I could see that Nick had flipped to the page about the Nose. He took off his new forest green cap, brushed his hair back with his fingers, and replaced the cap. The guru hadn't come back yet. "First night in there," Trip went on, "these two brothers come up to me and they say, 'Say, you look like you some kind of faggot. You a homosexual? We going to get you tonight.'

"I wasn't going to wait for that. So, you know, I broke out the blade of my shaving razor, and I just laid there all night holding it up high, ready, you know, looking around. In the morning one of them goes to the warden and says, 'That dude's got a blade over there.' So they doubled my sentence to sixty days. I was almost glad to be in there though, you know, 'cause I had a lot of time to think, you know, about what I'm doing. I was getting in shape too. I got up to nine hundred push-ups a day. That's forty-five sets of twenty. Fifteen sets in the morning. Fifteen at lunch, and fifteen after dinner. I was drawing a lot too."

The manager came out at last—no graphics work now, but he'd keep Trip in mind.

Forty-one

"At a women's bathhouse in Morocco," Kyla told a group of farm apprentices at a party, "I had the most amazing experience, because you always just see Muslim women covered up and never get to talk to them."

A male carpenter from Napa Valley began to play a drum while Naomi cut me a slice of cheesecake and poured unfiltered organic apple juice into paper cups. She looked better than she had in a while and wore a new feathered necklace that Chris had given her. She mentioned that she and the baby would be leaving in a few weeks for the Oregon place. She'd get the big old farmhouse while Chris got the school bus ready for the trip.

"These women," Kyla went on, "like scrubbed me down, and I was so much paler than them and blond, and they were laughing because my hair was so knotted, and it was really mystical to see so many women naked and unveiled, with all of their hair down, tons and tons of really dark hair and breasts. And clouds of steam and everybody was soaping each other's bodies, touching each other all over for hours with just the warmest feeling of total acceptance."

The group was entranced. An anemic water-diva from Massachusetts had already begun to dress like Kyla, to wear her hair in the same way. A plump, blank-faced and nervous woman confessed to Kyla that she had, in a recent mushroom hallucination at Disneyland, seen herself as Kyla—light, thin, airy—beautiful.

One of the teachers at the farm had thrown the party. A shaman by profession, he'd grown up in England and had been educated in London. Out at the end of the Far West he'd found room to be himself. Around the plush carpeted house were clean new drums and little altars—statues of goddesses, symbols of the elements arranged in miniature medicine wheels, seashells, candles. His wife, an unemployed belly dancer, said she wanted to open a health food store.

I sat on a meditation pillow alone and watched my beautiful girlfriend tell more stories of sisterly love with dark-skinned others. Naomi breast-fed Nora and laughed at every one of Kyla's cadences. I could've sworn there was desire in her eyes, but knew I was prone to seeing such things. Kyla glanced over at me mid-sentence and looked concerned. From her look I realized I was grinding, pissed-off. Trying to see these little idiot fucking altars all around me as no more bizarre than the little ritual I'd fixated on for my own rite of passage. If sweetheart herb farmers were finding the warrior within, who was I chasing? The Psycho Overlord Conqueror of the Universe within?

The next day Kyla and I drove up the coast and had lunch at a restaurant on Highway 1 overlooking a windswept lagoon; I licked and sucked on barbecued oysters while she had carrot soup. Afterwards, we walked the foggy beach and talked about when we'd see each other again. My latest ambition seemed to upset her, even to disgust her. She also mentioned enjoying our time apart. She liked the solitude, the space, and felt like she was finally growing in ways she'd always wanted. She worried I was incurably skeptical of her new wisdom, that my mind was so linear it kept me from experiencing life fully.

"I don't know," I told her, "this Nose thing. Boy, is it big."

"What?" she asked.

I looked at her in surprise.

"What did you just say?" she demanded.

I repeated myself, and she asked what that had to do with anything we were talking about. "I'm leaving for Christopher's Gardenville place in a month," she said, without waiting for my answer. "He asked me again if you were coming." She picked up my right hand, which was fattened and calloused, covered with scabs. "I'm really, really excited about it, and I swear you'd love it. Chris is a pretty beautiful guy, too, even if he's a little conceited and spacy. I think you could learn a lot from him."

I gave it a last shot: "Climbing can't count as a vision quest, huh?"

She thought about it for a few paces and picked up a shard of sand-polished green glass. I wondered if when I had the Nose behind me I'd be able to relax about her utopian fantasies. Maybe I could keep her around, even mend some of the distance.

"Dan, I think it's great you've got something you're into," she said at last, shaking her head. "But it's so much about yang and victory. It's just so meticulous and aggressive and so self-oriented. You're not giving or producing anything."

How much did she want out of a mate? I agreed with her politics, liked to bake bread, was obsessed with nature, had no hang-ups about making love in meadows, was even willing to take occasional drugs with her, although I was sure I was getting gradually stupider because of it. What more could she ask for?

While she spun a long, smelly strand of seaweed over her head, I gave up the direct approach and asked more about what they were doing in school. Tried to make it clear I really wanted to hear, keep my interest from seeming clinical. She knew what I was doing and went along with it. She said they had class out in some fields once and talked about moon time, about changing their relationship with their period, dealing with cramps differently. Beth had urged them not to just stick a tampon up there and not wear white pants that day, but to wear homemade cloth pads and clean them out in a bowl so they could put the bloody water on their plants, give the blood back to the Mother.

"Don't dread your period," Beth had said, "celebrate it, turn inward, squat down and bleed in the earth, let it drip into the soil, skip the pill and feel the cramps, get in touch with the pain, change your idea of it."

"Why are you smiling?" Kyla asked.

"Nothing. Nothing. No, it just sounds wonderful."

"Out in the field," Kyla said, "we decided to give offerings to the trees. Beth had a quilted box with a woman made of cloth on top of it. You lift the lid and it's like her lap opens up . . . Dan, are you smirking?"

"No. Go on."

"So Beth keeps little shiny objects in there, like gemstones, and mineral eggs and symbols and stuff. We put them in these big holes in the trees that are like tree bellies or tree wombs."

A V of prehistoric pelicans floated on the cushion of air that rests inches off the ocean. They rose and fell with the swells as they drifted above them, never flapping their wings.

"It turns out," Kyla was saying, "this little girl who lives next door has a fairy she's created that lives in a little hole in the ground where the girl puts treasures and magic objects, so we all left gifts there to the fairy."

I had come out from a summer camp once to that same beach with all the other counselors to barbecue oysters and drink. I'd never been drunk before and fell asleep in the sand by the fire.

Kyla stood upright in the breeze, the tapestry she'd wrapped around her legs parted at her hip and flapped about. "We also made fire cider," she said, "which is this herbal combo that gets your body going. It's like garlic, cayenne, ginger, horseradish and onion, and I've made it before, but Beth says you can't just blend it, you've got to bury it in the earth for a month to get that energy and to get it really shaking. Most tinctures you shake once a day before you press them, but the fire cider you bury, and obviously it's shaking under there, so we sort of made a little ritual out of it. How does it shake under there? It just does. It gets moving. Shit happens under the ground, don't you think?"

I supposed I did, but didn't, really, although I thought I ought to be able to think so. The sand was coarse, made more of pebbles than grains. Waves swelled right up to the beach, dark green in the fog with veins of white, and boomed onto the sand in a muddy surge. A powerful under-tow sucked pebbles in tumbling lines down toward the water.

They'd made dolls one day, too, Kyla said, laughing out loud. She knew it was silly, hilarious even that she was mak-ing dolls at age twenty-two, but loved it nonetheless. Beth had brought cloth and beads and they used different colors to symbolize different things—red for fire and anger, blue for emotion. Then they filled the dolls with herbs—mug-wort in the doll's head for dreams, corn in its feet for groundedness. There were many jars of seeds and little feathers with magical powers.

"And we all ended up using every one," Kyla said, for a moment being ironic, "because of course every magical power's great and of course you'll want passion and love and brainpower."

"Who wouldn't?"

We lay on the beach under a blanket until well after dark. When we'd gotten cold, wet and covered with sand from rolling around, we dressed and ran back to her car. On the way she asked me to be careful on the Nose. We drove back to the farm with the top down and the heater turned up. Kyla held my hand as she huddled under Guatemalan blankets and smiled with her eyes closed in the wind.

Forty-two

Central Valley slaughterhouses reeked with the blood of a million cattle as Aaron floored it toward Yosemite. Why that guy was so committed to speeding, I'll never understand. The roar of the wind against his thin-walled, rattling Bug made conversation a struggle. For long, carsick hours I huddled near the map light under the dash and looked over the topo. Tried to break it down, see a series of manageable tasks. The Nose of El Capitan. Wide-open sky up there . . . thousands of vertical feet . . . outer space—no beginning, no end, too big to get bearings. So big that from below, climbers were really visible only with binoculars, and even then not well. To the naked eye, climbers were specks like grains of pepper on a dining table, easily lost in the blotches and shadows of the wall. The biggest and most famous rock-climb in the United States, in some ways the longest pure rock-climb in the world. Certainly one of the greatest. Thirty Harley-Davidsons passed us at eighty like a swarm of bellowing fireflies in the dark.

"Because it's huge," Aaron yelled over at me, "that's why." He rolled down his window and his hair whipped around his head so much I wondered how he could drive.

They said storms, though very unlikely at this time of year, were inconceivably wild; climbers had died up there in every season, of heat exhaustion in January and hypothermia in July. Warren Harding took six months of sieging to pull off the first ascent; teams of climbers ferried supplies up and down fixed ropes to keep the effort underway. Dad had talked about it for years, knew all the history. Guys at Berkeley bouldering areas and at the shop held endless El Cap rap sessions; I'd wanted to track down some veterans to annotate our route map, but Aaron wouldn't allow it. Thought we ought to just do the thing. Every visiting foreign climber dreamed of pulling it off, and often came through the shop to ask about it. Aaron didn't even want to discuss it. He just hauled his little car around mountain turns and occasionally told me to relax. We were up in the evergreens now, their pointy tops flitting past at the border of the stars. The air cooled and I zipped up my parka.

To be able to say I'd climbed the Nose? Maybe never need to do another wall? Jesus, just to have done one, the big one. I could stick to short, sunny routes in the Meadows after that and get more into surfing. Aaron yelled something. I asked him to repeat it.

"You can't just want to have done it."

"What does that mean?" I asked.

"Just what I said."

Sickle Ledge marked the first real destination on the route proper. Four pitches off the ground, standard procedure involved climbing up the meandering route to it the day before your intended blast-off, then fixing ropes straight back to the ground. This let you haul your obscenely heavy haul bag directly up steep, smooth terrain instead of along the route itself. From there we'd go to famous El Cap Towers at the halfway point to spend our first night; then on to airy Camp Six high in the upper dihedral, and off the day after that.

Amazing to look at a route map of thirty-two pitches and start on number one. Then, an hour later, number two. Another hour of hard work, mistakes, hassles and bleeding hands, and you look at number three. And the wind won't leave you alone, pushing you around, yelling in your ears, making your eyes run. Now it's past lunchtime, we haven't even had a haul bag with us, and we've gone four pitches. I tried to work methodically and not look up. Just keep plugging away, do the small tasks, don't worry about the long haul, it'll all come together over time. Aphorisms all afternoon. Man, that wall was big. It swam around while we climbed like a gargantuan skyscraper drifting across stationary clouds. When we'd finished the rappels to the ground a grizzled guy with wild dark hair and too-tan wrinkled skin stood staring at us; lean, dirty, wearing sunglasses. Huge rack of iron aid-gear hanging off his shoulder. Thick southern accent. We asked what he was coming off.

"Sea of Dreams." Aaron glanced at me: a death route. And Aaron's ultimate ambition.

"How was it?"

"Scary." He watched our faces from behind his shades. The Camp 4 parking lot had enough light at night to pack, so we parked there and organized. Fluorescent lights at the gas station buzzed in the night while a young Spanish man wept in one of the phone booths. A small schnauzer licked at his bare toes. I made some last phone calls home. I told Dad we were going for it and that I'd be careful. I felt like I'd announced plans to go to Mars, return date uncertain. Just stepping off the planet. Guys rarely said, "I'm going to do the Nose." More common was something like, "I'm going up on the Nose." Not a thing one did, but rather a place one went.

I also got this terrible idea that precooked falafel sandwiches would be great fuel for three days of lunch and dinner. A man Aaron knew from Earth Island Institute walked by, kicking up dust, talking about how some fashion magnate had agreed to give Ancient Forests International five million dollars to buy five hundred thousand acres of rain forest in Peru to create an international park that nobody can go to.

Back to the wall at midnight to sleep at the ropes: a bushwhacking nightmare of wandering among low trees with crippling loads on our backs. At last at the base of that moonlit ghost of a monolith, we found our lines and hung the bag a pathetic five feet up, worried about the cloud of falafel odor surrounding it and how it might attract scavenging Yosemite bears. I don't think I slept more than an hour with all that stone browbeating me. It struck me as hilarious that a mind could so fixate on inanimation.

Then the alarm went off and I heard something falling. I stumbled and rolled over Aaron to get behind the tree. On a wall that big you can hear something coming a long time before it hits. The sound again, then just a light tap nearby. Probably just a stopper. And there we were, sitting in the dark before dawn, with so much left to do. I pulled on my rock shoes, strapped on knee pads, taped my hands, put on my harness, put on my daypack, then attached my jumar ascension clamps to the hanging rope.

I humped upwards, bouncing a bit as the rope stretched under my pull. Cool morning and a shadowless, growing light—the ground inched away below. It was sweaty, nauseating work, in weather so mild that the mountaineer's sense of entering the belly of the beast, of the jaws of death with howling storms and avalanches, was too remote to even conjure. The wall was just there, warmed by the California sunshine. Climb it or don't.

At about the halfway point to Sickle Ledge I heard another party at the base where Aaron and I had started the day before. By the time I'd jugged up the two remaining pre-hung ropes—in the space of half an hour—they'd led and followed clear to Sickle. A blond guy in a tank top was panting on the ledge when I got there. Trying to break their own record of six hours three minutes, he said. For the whole route? Yeah, the whole route. Going for under six hours. His partner appeared—tall, skinny, round glasses— a sweet, Dungeons & Dragons-looking kind of guy:

"Here's the gear. Go. We're still holding at twelve minutes a pitch." And he was gone. Aaron and I hoped to stay steady at an hour per pitch—a respectable pace for good, strong climbers. I was left standing in the quiet, clipping and unclipping, trying to remember what needed doing, staying calm, moving from small task to small task.

A sound like an Apache attack helicopter roared overhead and as I looked up two black objects appeared against the dawn's deep blue. No idea what it was. Suddenly the forms started to ripple and expand. Then, "Whoooooooooo-wheeeee!" Two men in parasails drifted toward El Cap meadow, flying in the morning's peace, steering toward a clearing close to the trees. Base jumpers. From the top of the Captain they'd sprinted for the edge of the Dawn Wall—and jumped.

Someone high above cursed. I could see the speed-climbers scampering away. Aaron arrived, exhausted from dealing with a tangled rope. We organized for an hour, got our ropes sorted out, had a few bagels, then started climbing. One hold at a time, we crawled up the route and slowly the wind began to blow. The granite felt no different from the granite on small climbs, and soon we were just moving. I started to loosen up and think we might make it.

Later in the morning a party of Mormons closed on us from behind. Soon one of them caught up with me while Aaron climbed ahead. Hanging in a huge smear of fresh shit from a faster party, he pointed out that our haul bag seemed awfully damp, like maybe a water jug had burst.

When I'd jumared up to Aaron, I noticed he'd only clipped the rusty old permanent gear and the frayed webbing connecting it. We couldn't possibly know how long it had been there. If all the anchors were this bad and Aaron wouldn't back them up, we were going to be on acres of thin ice. The wind suddenly gusted harder and I tried to lean flat against the wall, to get my head out of it. But even with my eyes closed it roared in my ears.

Well into the afternoon we were on a section called the Stovelegs—Harding had protected these long, perfect cracks with big pitons hacked off junkyard stoves. Suddenly, however, it felt like we were on El Capitan—the vistas were hard to believe, and the trees were shrinking quickly; we hadn't stood on a decent ledge for hours, and my harness had started to cut into my sides. So exposed to wind; and Aaron seemed nervous, wasn't climbing as well as usual. On an easy crack I resorted to pulling on gear; something about thirty pounds of rope and thirty pounds of gear made movement a nasty struggle. The bag now had a steady drip. Clouds drifted overhead and I called down to Aaron,

"Storm coming?"

"No dude. Puffballs. No storm."

"You sure?"

The sheer volume of the task ahead made the end seem unbearably remote; I could have sworn we were steadily slowing down. Tremendous spaghetti now—the haul line tangled throughout the anchor lines, the lower-out line for the haul bag a mass of spontaneously generated knots. Three more days and we'd have to function perfectly to stay safe. While Aaron led a hard off-width for me—I was already too scared, needing a break—the older Mormon talked about his Porsche 944 and his new Puerto Rican wife, what a little doll she was. He whistled softly and rolled his eyes, said he's going down to Puerto Rico, hang out in the sun, drive around in that Porsche, damn. Said I should see her. What a peach. He'd been up on this wall twice before. Both times to right here. Yep, he said, first time stormed off. Second time his partner short-circuited. Then had to skip a season because he broke his tib and fib when his motorcycle hit a patch of gravel. Now he was back, going to make it. Happy for diversion, I asked if the plan was to get the Nose in before having babies.

"I'm not having babies," he said, laughing and winking. "I'm fixed." Wearing a powder-blue wind jacket and baseball cap, he had a perfectly trimmed silver beard, pale skin, blue eyes.

In that outrageous wind, in the tangled ropes, fear over funky anchors and abject terror at the idea of getting lost up in the vast spaces of that wall (good God it's big) I started to wonder. Water now fairly poured from the bottom of the bag. If we'd lost more than a gallon . . . they said dehydration was almost as crippling as hypothermia. Lovely Kyla and that lush green farm seemed all right. Did I have to do it? That kind of abstraction had always struck me as ridiculous, as a kind of integrity best avoided. But I also knew the power of fear to affect judgment. After all, we were still moving, unhurt.

Aaron suggested we rest, have a look inside the bag. He pulled out a falafel sandwich and we both tried to get our heads out of the wind. The howling in my ears spoke with forked tongue of weather on the move, danger, instability; it threw off my balance. I talked to myself about maybe spending a night, seeing how I felt in the morning.

It's just rock climbing, no different. But shit, I could truly, honestly, no joke die. Folks who think the world's all in our heads should check out El Cap. And the falafel was virtually inedible.

No. Absolutely not. I shook all over and choked with fear, suddenly coming unglued. I couldn't talk. I'd walked into a world I was nowhere near ready for. There were steps of approach I should've taken, build-up climbs, an apprenticeship. Nick was absolutely wrong—I had no death wish at all, only a desire to do something worth doing. The spaces above seemed uncontrollably wild and vast and I hadn't nearly the self-confidence to navigate them. Aaron had just racked up and reached his hand into a crack to pull away.

"Can't do it, dude," I said. I heard my words like a spasm I chose not to resist.

"What?"

"The route. I want down."

"You're kidding."

I shook my head, tried to look convinced without letting him see my fear.

"You freaked about those clouds?"

I stared at him until he realized I just meant me, I was the problem. Desire had fled in a big hurry and I couldn't really explain it.

"You sure?" he asked.

I nodded, suddenly overjoyed at the decision, thrilled that I could give myself an out. He stared away at Sentinel for a while, then looked at his taped-up hands, at all the gear, at the crazy sweep of stone above.

Forty-three

During the long and painful rappel, disappointment mingled with elation at being both alive and freed from my stupid ambition. I touched ground and dropped everything: terra plata. A nervous young Brazilian man—beautiful with long hair—smiled and said, "Good job." Heroes home from the front. Conquerors just for considering it.

We were so spent we sat for a full hour before coiling ropes. We organized the gear sluggishly, with no motivation, taking no pleasure in it. As I stared back up at the route, already wondering what had been so frightening, Aaron caught me shaking my head.

"No shame," he said. "No shame."

We slept in the guerrilla spot and gorged on French toast and eggs in the morning. Spent the whole next day out in the meadow watching the wall. The Mormons were taking forever. Rain clouds threatened and we both hoped it would pour—at least we'd be able to say it stormed like hell the next day. A rope on the Dawn Wall was being blown completely horizontal. Three Japanese men started off to do the Shield. Exhaustion kept us on our backs all day.

Regret crept in—the Big Stone. I'd been on it; I'd done fine on a quarter of it. The ultimate climb. It was just rock climbing. I would have been able to say, "I did the Nose."

"Who gives a shit?" Aaron demanded.

While we drank beers in the bar our waitress said Euroclimbers had been freaking out and bailing off the Nose all spring. She got a big tip. After burritos we went into the Ahwahnee to look at magazines and buy chocolate. Walking around that palace we saw the skinny speed-climber from the wall.

"Yeah, I bailed three times before I got up the Nose," he said. "You shouldn't feel bad. Just keep at it. We saw you guys doing that traverse on pitch seven. You looked fine."

"Where'd you see us from, El Cap towers?"

"No, from the ground."

Aaron flinched, then looked away and sighed. They'd climbed twenty-nine pitches and walked to the ground in the time we'd climbed four pitches.

"Twelve minutes per pitch?"

"Yeah. We did the route in like nineteen pitches with a two-hundred-foot rope. It was pretty intense. My partner did the summit overhangs with a piece of webbing and a 'biner tied around each wrist and he just swung from bolt to bolt clipping them. He basically did like twenty one-arm pull-ups."

Off to the woods for the night, then on home. We rattled back through the foothills and into the Central Valley, bouncing on that old suspension. Aaron barely talked, except to say he still had to find Amanda. I didn't even ask why he figured she felt anything for him; I could tell the uncertainty was the point. Catastrophic depression set in. Aaron hadn't been spooked in the least, and Dad said he'd loved every second of being on Half Dome. So many people had made it up the Nose, I figured I'd just found out what a coward I was. I thought maybe I should bail around the world, travel for a while.

In front of my apartment Tracy walked up while I unpacked. I talked about the Captain for a moment, then about misery and failure. Wallowing. I knew I'd be depressed for a week and would have a hard time getting out of bed. I asked Tracy what was new with him. He said his dad had come down with HIV dementia: the virus had penetrated the blood-brain barrier and would gradually consume his personality and cut off vital functions. Tracy'd been reading Whitman to him in the hospital.

Forty-four

When Mom showed up at Royal Coffee, wearing jeans and a blue cotton sweater, she put an old drum down on my sidewalk table and said she'd be right back. She walked inside for a latté and a morning bun. I waited in the sunshine and tapped away in no particular rhythm. The drum was a chunk of tree-trunk stretched tight with caribou hide, filthy from twenty years of handling. Chris had been teaching Kyla some drumming patterns and she'd told me on the phone how much she loved it. She'd never been much into dancing, had never really felt anything from pop music, but something about hand-percussion woke up her desire to move. I'd asked Mom to bring this old thing because I was meeting Kyla at the beach and I knew she'd love it. It didn't sound great, but it looked truly ceremonial.

"You grew up with that drum," Mom offered when she sat down. Her brown hair had streaks of gray that matched her eyes. She looked at me like its story was loaded. "You want to talk about spirituality?" she said, nodding her head. "A little boy made that drum who spent his whole life in the wilderness in the Alaska range. His parents were friends of mine who homesteaded out there in the late fifties." She dipped a piece of bun in her coffee and recrossed her legs. I remembered the couple from when I was a kid. We'd gone out to visit them as a family when they lived in a meadow in Marin county. My sister and I both thought their kids were pretty weird. I could see Tracy and Brynn walking up the street.

"Their son," Mom continued, "was the most beautiful little brown-eyed boy. And he made that drum when he was only twelve. Do you know he personally shot everything he ate from the day he could fire a gun? You ought to tell Kyla and her vegetarian friends about these people. I was barbecuing burgers once for you and your sister when Frank, the father, gave me this big rap about how agriculture and domestic meat were the seed of all corruption. So he took his whole family out into the Alaskan wilderness and they ate nothing but wild meat—mostly caribou." Something in Mom rebelled against orthodoxy; she tolerated no one who willingly occupied a moral higher ground, however just.

"One afternoon in the late fall," she continued, "a few hours after the last mail plane of the season took off from their lake, that little boy spilled a huge pot of boiling water all over his back and chest." Brynn caught my eye and waved. Mom looked up and waved back, sitting back in her chair resigned to an interruption. I actually wanted to see them, but the visit didn't materialize—Tracy was buying a banana at the fruit stand across the street.

Mom leaned forward again and rested her elbows on the table. A meat truck double-parked and began disgorging boxes of organic chickens. "They were really out in the

woods," she said, meaning they weren't New Age poseurs,
"And Eliza thought her boy was going to die. Frank was out
hunting alone, and there was nothing either of them
could've done anyway. She told me she sat next to her weep-
ing little child and concentrated all of her being on bringing
another plane."

My friend the chemist's son sat down nearby and
flipped open his Powerbook. He could see we were having a
conversation and didn't interrupt.

"That boy was literally dying he was in so much pain
and he was going unconscious when Eliza heard a noise.
She told me she covered her boy's mouth and listened
through the walls of their split-log cabin. It was always
really windy by their lake and she could barely hear anything. But then she heard it again. She ran like mad out of
the cabin with her boy in her arms and sure enough, a little
Piper Cub had landed on the lake. She jumped in her
canoe, paddled out there, and climbed right inside. She
screamed over the roar of the engines to fly to Anchorage,
and they took off."

Mom talked on about how the pilots were a couple
Eliza knew who also lived out in the mountains—an Eskimo woman and an American man—friends Eliza hadn't
seen in years. Mom's latté got cold and I finished her but-
tery, sweet roll while she told the story about how for the
entire flight they all sat quietly under the din of the propel-
ler and how when they got to Anchorage, Eliza ran for a taxi
to the hospital without saying a word.

"Not until she got back from the hospital," Mom said,
"and her boy's life was saved and the couple was gone, did

she realize she had no idea why her friends had landed in the first place. It was fully a year until Eliza saw that Eskimo woman again and asked." Mom took a sip of her cold latte and put her hands between her knees.

"The woman said to Eliza, 'I don't know.' She apparently chuckled a little and said, 'Oh, we were passing over and I thought there might be trouble. My husband wanted to know how I could know such a thing, but I said, 'Let's just go look.' Eliza was as mystified as you or I would be, so she asked her friend if she felt stuff like that a lot. The woman just shrugged her shoulders like it was nothing and said, 'Sometimes.'"

The chemist's son had stopped typing and was working on the *New York Times* crossword when his girlfriend joined him. A box fell out of the meat truck and burst open on the pavement. Three shiny wet chicken carcasses rolled into the gutter.

"You know, Danny," Mom said, "that boy drowned up there when he was fifteen and his father Frank died in a plane accident the next year. Can you believe Eliza stuck it out alone with her daughter for another whole winter? Finally she came back to San Francisco. She never felt she could keep away the wolves and bears by herself." Mom looked at her watch and realized she was late for work. She leaned over and kissed me, then walked off down the street.

Sitting on the smooth-pebbled sand of Muir beach, her hair completely re-corn-rowed and already dreading, Kyla mentioned the reading with Beth: "She says I need to give

birth to myself before giving birth to anybody else." Kyla
threw back her hair and laughed at her own expense. "So I
guess that means I'm in labor. I'm kind of getting into
magic, too."

Kyla bit her lip and looked at me as if with a challenge.
She picked up the drum and patted, thumped and tapped
while two friends of hers, back from three months in India,
lit a bowl of homegrown with a magnifying glass—the purest of ingredients, the purest of heat. Kyla had learned
some pretty sophisticated rhythms; as she worked them
out, her friends talked about bodies rotting in the luggage
racks of the trains on the way to the Ganges at Varnasi and
about eating curried everything, curried breakfast. We
watched pale people swim in a freezing, pounding shore
break with fog just off shore. Two surfers in thick black wet-
suits bobbed like ghost seals in the mist, their eyes fixed out
to sea.

We pulled out of the gravel beach parking lot and
passed a group of octagonal redwood houses on hillsides
overgrown with blooming heather, then the Pelican Inn—
brought timber by timber from England. The road wound
up a grassy slope above Green Gulch Farms, a self-suffi-
cient Zen monastery. I'd been there when little with my
family—my parents sat za-zen while my wild, teasing sister
and I wandered around in the fields and threw rocks. Now
people were harvesting lettuce, working together, no wet-
backs. Kyla beamed.

I looked at the dashboard and noticed a change—it
had always had sage and other herbs, but now there was a

new collection—a pelvis bone, a yellow feather, the second crystal Rain had given her—also broken—and a dried bunch of seaweed.

"Magical?" I asked.

"Actually," she responded, "elemental."

We rounded a bend and came in sight of weekenders harvesting tomatoes. "The feather for air," she said, "the crystal for earth, the nori for water."

"No fire?"

"No fire."

Forty-five

No sound disturbed the natural quarry below Half Dome. In predawn light, I smeared cream cheese on a flattened onion bagel and looked out over the whole of Yosemite Valley. A surprising view from so high above, from a place I had until now only looked up to: the right wall of the valley was an ordered row of forms: Washington Column, the Royal Arches, Yosemite Falls, the Three Brothers and El Capitan; the left—Glacier Point, Sentinel Rock and the Cathedral Group. Even at five a.m. the air held midsummer heat; dried sweat and dust caked my skin from the previous night's approach and my shoulders still ached from the load. As I ate, my own stench overpowered the blandness of the bagel. I chewed slowly and looked around at the Northwest Face—there was something that baffled me about that wall's beauty. So out of human scale and yet so well formed, so sculpted. A vast field of fallen boulders lay along its base, like so many sculptor's shavings from a work in progress.

Nick organized the haul bag quickly, and soon we had lifted off. Half Dome wasn't so much smaller than El Cap—twenty-six pitches by comparison to thirty-two—but somehow it seemed far more manageable, less steep and less difficult. We climbed steadily and well on familiar gray granite, deep inside corners and cracks. Perhaps because the sun didn't strike the Northwest Face until noon, and the air remained still, the wall felt like a vast and empty indoor cathedral. We ran our rope systems, made moves well within our abilities, and were soon well off the ground. Sound took on a singular quality—even with Nick a hundred feet above, every little tap of metal on stone, every scuffle of a shoe, his deep breaths and occasional remarks—each and every noise echoed alone like lonely footsteps in a huge stone hall.

At a ledge a few hundred feet up, light just breaking into the sky, I prepared for my first lead of the morning. Nick sat against the rock and looked blankly out over the high country; the haul bag was perched next to him, leaning against the wall. I dismantled the pulley system and clipped the haul line into my harness to take it up with me. Then the haul bag teetered back, Nick looked up and reached for it too late, and then it was gone. Well over a hundred pounds. We both grabbed reflexively for the rope; my hand caught it and instantly slammed back against the rock and split open. The rope burned skin off my thigh as coils flipped off the ledge. The bag had a hundred and sixty-five feet to fall before it would impact my harness. Nick and I stared at each other and waited for the inevitable. I wrapped my hands around the anchor webbing and held on.

The jolt slammed me down into the ledge, then stopped. My harness had held the fall. Nick's knuckles were raw. The bag was intact. My right hand bled down onto my wrist. So close to blowing the whole climb. We looked at each other in disbelief: had he forgotten to clip it to the anchor? Had I unclipped the wrong knot? It didn't matter much, and we barely spoke of the incident; we just hauled the bag back in and went on with our work.

Hours and hours of quiet climbing in the still shade; hauling, belaying, jumaring, climbing, hauling, clipping and unclipping, reclipping and untying, backing up and re-organizing, rambling up across the tower toward the wall. Alternately lost in the sheer pleasure of motion and then drifting in the emptiness of waiting. Sitting on some little ledge high over the world and just staring. I never had many thoughts at belay ledges on long climbs, I didn't ruminate on what lay below or come to new clarity about my life. The task so absorbed me and the fatigue so calmed me that I really just looked, and occasionally even just saw.

We'd exchange a few words here and there about equipment or ropes or which way the route went, but I loved the feeling that very little needed saying. We'd been climbing together for a while and knew each other well. Nick had decided that cities were crowded with psychic static; he said in a pause at a ledge that high places got him above the web of noise, especially his own. And for me Half Dome, unlike El Capitan, was charted territory. My father had been here, had climbed every inch of this rock and saw it as one of his happiest experiences.

Late in the day, at pitch eight of twenty-six, Nick led out across narrow but walkable ledges and began the Robbins Traverse, where Royal Robbins had taken the first ascent team off the tower and out onto the Northwest Face. Then, with my feet in aiders I moved as fast as I could on ancient, strange-looking bolts—fat nails driven into spread-out sheaths. Only a few of the bolts had hangers, and even those were only partially bent pieces of aluminum. The last of the bolts was so bent out of the rock it was hard to imagine much was left inside.

In the early evening we reached our bivouac ledge at pitch eleven—a thirty-foot-long, three-foot-wide notch formed by a massive exfoliating flake.

"Sweet, huh?" Nick said.

After a short break, we decided to fix a line or two ahead so we could get a good start in the morning. I scrambled up to where blocks lay wedged in the opening of a chimney. Stepping across them I could hear sand and pebbles drop into the chasm. Somewhere in the darkness below, light leaked in from a crack. My pitch went well—easy aid, t.c.u.'s, fixed pieces in a beautiful white corner to the left of the chimney.

I leaned back and looked about. The crack was lined with old fixed pins; the face to either side was blank. As Nick started leading the next pitch, it became clear how tired he was—too much pro, thrashing around, stepping clumsily. At last he hung from a piece and looked back down at me with a smile.

"I'm out of here," he said.

"The whole route?" I couldn't believe my ears.

"Relax, bro. Just this pitch. Let's eat." We slid back

down our skinny ropes and stumbled across blocks back to
the vaguely comfortable part of the ledge. Everything came
out of the bag. Feet came out of sweaty, torturous rock
shoes and into clean socks. No point in so much as standing up—nowhere to walk, and everything an arm's reach
away. I pulled out our dinner and started getting depressed.
Sure I'd learned from the falafel, but we'd bought our food
in a Berkeley health food store, and had gotten on a clean
fuels kick. So we had nothing but dried this, dried that,
bread, cheese, nuts, seeds—nothing that felt like a fitting
meal after a hard day's work.

"Dude." Nick had his head under a rock, was reaching
for something. "Check it out. Treasure!" Four full cans had
been abandoned by some retreating party—blueberries,
clam chowder, Spaghettios, Dinosaurs with Meatballs.
Stunning good fortune—the ultimate Wall Food. I couldn't
believe I hadn't thought of cans before. Nick demanded the
Spaghettios so I gladly took the Dinosaurs. The fat had
congealed beautifully in the top of the can and I scooped it
into my mouth with an old piton. The blueberries occupied
nearly an hour as we sucked them down one by one.

A red glow rose out of the horizon and Yosemite Valley
three thousand feet below softened and seemed of a piece,
a valley proper. The distinct monoliths fell into a pattern of
overlapping slopes and walls. Darkness filled the Valley
from below as the harsh white of sun on granite faded into
soft, deep grays. Lights appeared, marking Curry and
Yosemite Villages. Faint car headlights crawling through
the trees actually looked homey and pleasant.

I'd always thought that bivies up that high should be wild, dangerous, somehow violent and disorderly. Nothing could have been farther from the truth. The wind stopped and the Valley's warm air rose as a soft breeze. No Valley tour busses roared, no traffic honked and smoked. No sound, no wind. Just warm air. Darkness obscured the wild exposure of our perch; it seemed a natural, even exquisite place to be.

I flaked ropes between blocks to make a bed, grinning like an idiot, almost crying with pleasure at the thought of sleep. My back, legs, arms, neck and chest burned sore; my hands were swollen, raw and scabbed. My extra clothing filled another spot, and the tent fly filled another. When at last I lay down I felt so heavy that rolling over and dangling in the void never occurred to me as a danger. I sank into the crevice in the rocks, comfortably lodged. But for a full hour after dark, I couldn't sleep. There was too much beauty to see, too striking and unique a view, so much precious sky. A perfect place attained by perfect means, by adequate struggle. Each time I began to fade, I wanted a last look; I whispered the whole scene out loud to myself, panting lightly as I spoke, mouthing the colors, the feeling of the warmth, the unbelievable quiet and stillness and my own attendant tiredness. I told myself the whole scene again and again to remember everything.

I opened my eyes in the middle of the night, that vast wild wall just a quiet, immobile place. The full moon, out of sight behind Half Dome, washed the sweeping granite apron of Glacier Point in cold white light. And then I realized what was before me: a moonshadow of Half Dome framed in the middle of the glow, a perfect projection of its curves on the apron. It occurred to me that these mountains always etched themselves across one another by sun and by moon, by shadow, dawn and dusk, and that for that moment on that night I lay with a blessed point of view between. Soon the shadow blurred and merged with the wider brushing of moonlight; before the moon itself rose into sight from behind the dome, I had fallen asleep.

Forty-six

When Nick's watch alarm beeped, the sky had iced over with light and the full moon had faded. I sat up in my sleeping bag and turned so my back was against the wall and my feet off the edge. We looked about for a while, faced once again where we were. Nick fished out our ration of bagels. I drank a whole liter of water mixed with electrolyte supplements. We were slow getting moving, but when we were both well awake, stretched, and warmed, we packed the terrific mess back into the haul bag and started climbing.

I felt like a fish on a line as I thrashed up our fixed ropes in a flaring chimney. For the first lead of the day, I groveled into a miserable fissure and lost confidence—aiding behind an expanding flake at the back of another chimney, I could barely turn my head around because of my helmet. Loose rock threatened to fall and kill Nick. I asked him to lower me down to clean a piece because the rope drag was stopping my upward motion.

"You can't just haul enough up?" Nick asked. "Come on, just try to haul it. It'll take forever to lower you." I looked around, already drained, worn out, tried to pull some more rope and couldn't. I got planted on a small ledge and did a full leg-press—a foot of rope came. Another press, another foot, and then I could build the anchor and relax. The day went as smoothly as the one before, and Nick and I began to talk and yell at each other, to laugh at what an absurdity it was.

We reached our bivouac—Big Sandy Ledge—at 3:30 with a storm gathering in the high mountains. We'd just dropped our gear on the ledge and sat down when three climbers popped up and hooted with delight at the sight of the approaching clouds—without bivy gear, rain gear, or food. They'd left the car at Curry Village at 9:00 a.m. that same day and had walked eight miles and climbed seventeen pitches since: bearded, sweating, psychotic super-hardmen having the time of their lives.

I admitted to one of them that I thought Nick and I might be in for a wild night on the ledge—looked like a big storm coming in; lightning flashed in the distance.

"But you'll have the greatest story to tell," he said, looking around at the sky, "and the bettys'll just be like 'give me your throbbing member!'" He was gone. Up the cracks called the zigzags. For a few hours later we could hear them yelling at each other.

With hours to kill till dark we sat on the ledge and stared, peed on different terraces, looked off into the sun for hours, watched a slow changing of the day, took turns shitting into paper bags and hurling them into space. Nick didn't even clear the ledge. Quite a mess. The storm moved overhead and deep booms and cracks sent us scampering for rain gear. Lightning charged into peaks; a black curtain of rain deluged Tenaya Canyon only a half-mile away. Nick giggled with nervous anticipation, apparently hoping for the thrill. We were well anchored down, had plenty of warm clothing and rain gear, and these storms rarely lasted more than a few hours. So let us have it. Blow us off the mountain.

And then the storm pulled back, just like that, and left us with a long beautiful afternoon. Sleep was again difficult because of the beauty of the night. I watched meteors, picked out constellations, leaned over to look at the valley again and again, thinking about my dad sleeping here. We woke up late, had a slow breakfast, and mosied up the zig-zags. After an hour and a half, we reached Thank God Ledge, which ran left for fifty feet. I'd seen pictures of my dad on Thank God Ledge, crawling like a lowly rat. Rather undignified. I'd bet him ten dollars I'd walk the whole thing. Nick got out the camera.

I walked right out there, no sweat. Shuffling along like a man. I could swear the ledge started narrowing a bit, but I kept walking just the same. The wall was pretty vertical above and below, and the valley floor was almost four thousand feet beneath my feet, but I just put one foot in front of the other. After ten feet or so, I turned to face the wall—spread my arms out flat against it and shuffled sideways with my cheek pressed flat—just to be safe. I mean, after all, at least I was still behaving like a biped. Five feet later, I sank right down to my knees and never looked back. The hell with it. Nick shot three frames of my retreating behind.

As we approached the summit, a few tourists looked down and waved. Unlike great Alpine peaks—snowy pinnacles in the stratosphere, the tops of Yosemite walls feel more like endings than goals; they remind you that the great part was being on the route, not, as Aaron would say, having done it. At last I scrambled up a rather mundane series of ramps and stood on top. Hikers who'd come up the cable staircase milled about. A startled teenage girl in cutoff Levis and a bikini top looked at my haggard face and said,

"Did you just come up that way?"

Great question. God, what a good question. Thank you so much for asking that question. "Well, ah, yes. Now that you mention it, I did."

She looked at me, then off the edge.

"Rad," she said. She spun on her heels and walked away, apparently having changed the channel.

On that high mesa of exfoliating granite, overweight marmots scavenged in unattended backpacks and the twenty or thirty people sitting around spoke quietly as if in a museum. A wind blew across the summit and out into the air over the Valley. Kids had their pictures taken on the diving board—a thin block that stuck straight out over the abyss. Nick lay on his belly and looked over the edge back down at the route. He yelled at me to join him, but I couldn't do it—too acute a sense of gravity.

The eight miles home were all downhill, and we ran almost the whole way, fast and stumbling, trying to make the showers before closing. Down the mist trail—steep riprapping, pounding on the knees, the fabulous torrent of Nevada Falls and the green meadow at its base—utterly unlike the surrounding plants. Vernal Falls was a wild column of water framed by moss and ferns, and its staircase trail, absolutely paved, suggested an Inca trail. At last, into the human zoo of Curry Village for showers. After washing off the whole experience, we went to the Loft Restaurant, where a Dutch milkmaiden of a girl served us hamburgers.

"Why you guys so thirsty?" she asked. "Half Dome? The Regular Route? Oh yeah, my boyfriend and I did a one-day winter ascent. It was so great."

We slept in our clean cotton T-shirts and jeans in the back of the truck. Coffee milkshakes at ten a.m., and then back to Berkeley. A Big Wall.

Forty-seven

Just as I finished the last lines of *Huckleberry Finn*, I heard footsteps in the hallway, then keys in the lock. I put down the book and Kyla walked into the apartment crying. A black leather band held back her mass of tight little blond braids and her face was red and swollen. She coughed and shook as she wept, and I could tell the crying had been going on for a long time, maybe the whole drive up. She dropped her purple Tibetan knapsack on the hardwood floor and sat down at the end of our futon.

"I can't keep coming back here," she said. She shook her head and wouldn't look at me. "I still cry for every homeless person. I'm going to Oregon. I want to be on that bus." She'd told me that much before, so I asked why things were any different. She looked at me like I'd accused her of adultery, then said, "Our paths are walking in parting ways." She had a third crystal necklace in her fingers, was turning it over and pressing its point into her thumb. "Everything feels so heavy."

"Me?"

"Everything. Our whole apartment and even how

much you love me. It's like this big weight." Her hands fell away from the crystal and her palms lay open in her lap. I could still smell the chocolate chip cookies I'd made for her that afternoon. "It's all like a weight on me," she said. "I need to be lighter. I need to just live."

I couldn't think of much to say because it seemed so prescripted, so inevitable. I sat up in bed. She'd stopped talking, and I watched her pack some of her clothing. She stood for a moment in the middle of the room and wondered aloud what to do with her plants. She said she couldn't give them to me because I'd probably let them die. Everything else she'd have to put in storage. All the dried flowers, most of our pots and pans, our futon frame. She wanted nothing she couldn't fit in her Carmen Ghia, no attachments.

All that time together, cohabitational, like a practice run for the big mid-life divorce awaiting everybody. And it was over, just like that.

"Can we be friends?" she asked.

"Sure." Again, freedom without loss.

Before I let her leave, I made a pot of licorice tea and opened a window in the kitchen. I asked her to sit with me and tell me why, what had happened. She tried one of my cookies and looked out toward Mount Tamalpais. It was an Indian summer, fall coming on, the sun low over the Bay. She said she and Naomi had gotten really close; she even loved the baby more than any lover she'd ever had.

"I mean," she said, "don't take it personally, it's just something about the total acceptance of a baby. They don't have any preformed ideas of who you are."

Kyla and Naomi had formed a drumming circle to bring the local women into an empowering environment; more and more, Kyla felt this reality working for her. My willingness to dabble in it finally wasn't enough—she needed someone who could celebrate the path she was on and join in it. Not hold her back. Naomi had told Kyla that at last she too felt a sisterhood growing, something they could take with them to Oregon. I imagined that something in Kyla's freedom from responsibility drew the burdened Naomi to her.

Naomi's transient childhood, then her unexpected pregnancy; this man Chris . . . such a wonderful creator of togetherness he was, but so hard to pin down. I sipped from my mug and ate another cookie. I watched a breeze rustle the many treetops below my window.

"We did a lot of weeding together, too," Kyla said. "Me and Chris. We share a lot. And I've been feeling totally guilty about it because you're so jealous." I sucked on a chocolate chip and looked straight into her eyes. I very predictably asked if she'd slept with him.

"Fuck you," she said, wincing. "He's just really into experience. And even our whole desire to farm. He's really afraid Naomi's going to leave him when she gets too big for his little farmer's life. She's up in Oregon right now at the new place."

It didn't burn me up the way it should have, and I guessed that meant it was just as well she was leaving. I was a little confused though, because I'd always assumed the infidelity would be with Naomi. "No sexual thing at all?" I asked.

She looked into her tea and blew along its surface. "More with both of them," she admitted. She still didn't look up.

"Sex with both of them?"

Suddenly she turned red. "Why do you reduce everything to screwing? You know, you're stuck in really bullshit ideas of love."

She got up from the table and picked up her bag. I grabbed one of her boxes of clothes and followed her down the poorly lit hallway. The old elevator clacked into place and I slid back the telescoping iron door. I repeated my question as we stepped in.

"Dan," she said, "do you really want to hear about this?" She was earnest, and I could tell she actually wanted to tell me, that she wanted to think we had that kind of intimacy. Maybe she also needed to hear how it sounded. Without rancor, I told her I did want to hear about it, which was true.

"Chris called Naomi in Oregon last night. I didn't hear the conversation, but he told her I wanted to join the family. He told her I feel love for both of them."

The elevator door opened and we shuffled out to the street. She pulled down the top of the Ghia and put her knapsack in the passenger seat. I put the box in the little space in back. I could tell she was crying again, and without looking up she said she felt really positive about it all working out. She was meeting Chris at the Sykes Hot Springs

Trailhead first thing in the morning.

"Just the two of you?"

"This is going to sound weird to you, but it's not. It's just consummating what's building up between us," she said. She opened the driver's door. "It's not about sex. I promised myself I won't start anything sexual without Naomi. Even though he's really sure she won't mind."

As I stood there in front of my white stucco apartment building and thought about Tracy and Brynn and the chemist's son, it occurred to me that perhaps being a second wife appealed to Kyla. She could have babies, not support herself, and not have a man on her back wanting to get laid all the time. It might be perfect. After all, I was too rigid. I was too focused on climbing and some vague notion of middle-class success. Sure I loved wilderness, but I didn't have much interest in farming and I didn't really mind living in Berkeley. It was a great town. Chris, like her, didn't feel the need to figure out a comfortable living—he was concerned only with his connection to more ancient rhythms.

Kyla was in the driver's seat now and I stood barefoot in the street with my hands on her door.

"He's a dreamer," she explained as she started that old car's engine. "He's focused on community and on people being together. It's beautiful." She put the car in gear and I stood back. "What are you thinking?" she asked.

"You really want to know?"

"Yeah."

"That's the stupidest thing I've ever heard."

Forty-eight

Early in the morning I sat outside my building on milk crates full of climbing gear and finished a latté. The chemist's son screeched out of the parking lot in his VW Rabbit—top down, NWA on the stereo—gave a quick wave and headed for work. Right on schedule, the Bug came around the corner. We were going back to the Nose.

Aaron looked tired and a little thin, but he clearly thought something was funny.

"I went looking for her," he said.

"Who?" I carried a box over.

"Who do you think? Amanda." He leaned his forehead against the steering wheel and chuckled. "Hopped a train to Sacramento, hitchhiked up to the Cascades." Why he hadn't just driven, I didn't bother to ask.

"Well, tell me about it while you help me pack."

He did, and in a few minutes we were all loaded up. He had an empty six-pack under the dashboard—not like him at all.

"Dude," he said, starting the engine, "you got to sport the food."

"How's that?"

"Spent my absolute last twenty bucks on a great bottle of champagne."

"How come?"

"For Amanda. I knew if I didn't go all out, I didn't have a prayer. Girls are like that."

I climbed into the little bucket seat and Aaron pulled around the corner for more coffee and pastries. Soon we were flying along the freeway. It was getting to be time to make it up El Cap. If nothing went wrong—no bad weather, no other parties, no accidents—I knew we'd pull it off. I'd have climbed El Cap and could get on with my life. I had this sneaking feeling, though, that my whole year would fall apart if I blew it. I wasn't sure exactly how much it mattered to me, but I knew it was getting a little ridiculous.

As we sped over the Coastal Range, Aaron told me how a trucker dropped him near where Amanda might be. Aaron had read a Sierra Club bulletin article about some bear work going on out there, and had a hunch it was Amanda's group. "Bushwhacking through hellacious underbrush," Aaron said, "because I'd missed the trailhead." He changed lanes suddenly and the car bounced once in recovery. He shook his head and pursed his lips. "I also hadn't eaten for a full day."

This time I asked why, and he said he just hadn't thought about it. "But anyways, so I wasn't feeling too hot. And then it pissed rain all over me, and all I had was my jeans jacket and a down sleeping bag. No tent, no stove, no food at all. I was screwed, guaranteed to die." He changed lanes again and I exchanged mystified glances with a woman in a gray Honda.

"Slept like all night under some boulders," he said. Both hands clenched the steering wheel. "Totally miserable." I looked over at him—he did seem worn-out, and even a little spooked, like he'd lost weight. His hair was so unwashed it looked wet. I hadn't even had a chance to tell him about Kyla, how things were over between us. At that moment she was probably just shouldering her pack with Post-Colonial Chris. We sped down into Livermore as the morning began to warm.

"When I woke up, dude, my ass was hungry."

"On account of how you hadn't eaten?"

"Right. So I started walking. Bumped into a couple of ladies on horses." Aaron drank from his cup and bit the whole top off an applesauce muffin. Crumbs stuck to the coffee that had dripped into his stubble. Then he put the coffee between his legs and rubbed his eyes. "So, I ask this one lady, all polite, if she's seen some bear researchers." Aaron took another long sip and slowly shook his head as he swallowed.

"Yeah?" I asked.

"Yeah what?"

"So what'd she say?"

"Oh, well, she just goes, 'Yeah, I seen 'em.' And she just stares at me. Looks me up and down. I'm like looking around going, 'Well, ah . . . where you seen 'em?' She goes, 'You looking for Amanda?'" Aaron looked over at me with raised eyebrows, stunned. I could feel a bad end coming.

"I couldn't believe it," Aaron continued, finally looking back at the highway. "So I just looked right at her and said, like it was nothing, 'Yeah.'"

I fished the Nose route map from my jeans pocket and unfolded it while Aaron went on. If we could only get past the psychic wall of the Stovelegs.

"Outrageous. This lady seriously asked me if I was Amanda's boyfriend." This time I'd gotten our topo anno- tated; a few guys at the Berkeley rock gym had written tips and advice all over the sheet in an assortment of hiero- glyphics. Leaving nothing to chance.

"Go on," I said. "So you did the smart thing, right? And came back home where people love you?"

"No way. I was like, 'Of course I'm her boyfriend, who do you think I am? Just some weirdo wandering the moun- tains looking for her?' She kind of looked at me funny, too, 'cause I was so out of my head. I think she felt sorry for me. She even gave me a Malt-nut PowerBar after she told me where Amanda was. So I munched it and cranked up this ridge to where she was supposed to be."

Past the windmill forest once again, we paused for sta- tion identification, agreed with one another for the ump- teenth time that those whirling tax write-offs were unspeakably strange. I looked over the rack list again to make sure we had everything. Aaron wanted to go light, but I was trying to talk him into bringing some extra pro. He continued:

"My heart's fully pounding, and I must have looked awful 'cause I hadn't really eaten in two days, but I still had the champagne. And I knew Amanda'd feed me. She's the killer backcountry cook. Then I saw all these tents and this lady getting water from a stream. I asked her about Amanda, and she was like, 'Yup, right over in that tent.'"

I squirmed in my seat at what had to be coming. Aaron could barely keep from laughing himself.

"The tent was all zipped closed and everything," he said, biting his lip and shaking his head, "and I kind of heard some rustling inside."

"Bad sign."

"Terrible sign. Absolutely terrible sign. So I kind of said hello, and a second later the zipper opens a little and just her head pops out. But it was really her, totally gorgeous. But then, dude, I hear some guy inside go, 'Who is it?' and you know what she says?"

"Huh?"

"She looks back inside and goes, 'I don't know.' I was crushed. But hey, I'm sure I wasn't too recognizable after all I'd been through. But then she's like, 'Aaron?' And the first thing she asks is, 'What are you doing here?'"

I looked up from the topo. I practically had the thing memorized. "Good question, no?" I asked.

"Good question!? What the hell'd she think I was doing there? Passing through? But she disappears back inside for a sec and I hear more rustling, and then she climbs out. Just pulling up her pile pants. Dude, I wish I could tell you how hot she is. But anyway, I handed her the champagne and she like cracked up! I mean what's funny about that?" He turned and looked at me, eyes wide, mouth open.

"Nothing. Nothing at all. In fact, it's touching."

He nodded in total agreement and looked back to the road. Both hands on the wheel, trying to look deeply hurt and sensitive, but clearly on the verge of laughter. "She just holds the bottle and goes, 'How long you staying?' I was shattered. I totally wanted to cry."

"Bullshit."

"I'm serious. I wanted to cry. But I didn't."

"Good show."

"Nope, I just kind of stepped back and went, 'Well, I guess first thing in the morning.' I felt like such a jerk. So she let me have a little bit of their dinner and said if it to-tally poured rain and I was really, really cold, then I could sleep in the tent with them."

We raced past the slaughterhouses once again and I strained to see the Sierra. A mountain range that size dead ahead of us should've been visible, but agricultural dust and highway smog blurred even the next town.

"How about the champagne?" I asked.

"Well, they were the ones who had something to cele-brate, you know, so I offered it to them. Figured they could use it. They didn't want it though. So I went off into the woods by myself and drank the whole bottle."

"Bad move."

"Terrible move."

At a gas station parking lot in Manteca I saw four men in full black leathers pushing a fifth in denim around in cir-cles on a white Harley-Davidson trying to get it started.

Forty-nine

We fixed ropes to Sickle Ledge that very afternoon, and that evening we returned with the haul bag. Nearing the wall, we passed a party of three. They'd just given up, bailing, forlorn. They looked with bewilderment at the self-confidence with which we marched forward. We were going to pull that baby off while they sat in the bar and argued over whose idea it was to retreat. We walked quickly and wove through the trees with purpose. Like we knew exactly where we were going.

When we stepped up to the bottom of our ropes, ready to shoot up and sleep on Sickle Ledge, a German couple was just starting up. On our ropes. Embarrassed, they came back down. Young, clean and beautiful, they laughed nervously and asked if we would take their ropes up and fix them as we jumared. The woman had her frizzy blond hair in a bun and wore pink cotton aerobics tights, white tennies and a pink tank top. She was laughing at herself as she struggled to tie stirrups of the right length for her ascenders.

We took their ropes along with us and as I neared Sickle Ledge I noticed two more climbers just finishing the escape rappels we'd used last time—touching down in the talus, giving up. We had a divine evening of quiet rest on the ledge, eating candy, listening to two Frenchmen yell at each other in the middle of the Stovelegs. They had a long way to go to Dolt Tower and it was getting dark. I couldn't help but feel sorry for them—the emotional buildup is so great for such a route, and the letdown so painful. They'd come a long, long way to climb the Captain and now they were retreating without having made a good try of it. The weather was perfect, there was nobody ahead of them, they hadn't been hurt; they'd be furious with themselves when they got down. I could've told them all about it.

Aaron and I thrashed around to find somewhere to sleep—he found a spot longitudinally level, but laterally sloping in the direction of the void; I found one laterally level, but longitudinally easing me down onto Aaron's head. Nothing to do but plant my feet on his shoulder for the night, the outside shoulder so as not to pry him off. With the sun setting well out of sight behind valley walls, the dusk slipped through as a battery of colored spotlights shining on Middle Cathedral Rock. Clouds we couldn't see darkened and lightened fields of stone directly across from us. Then I heard one of the French climbers yelling in a tone that sounded aimed at us.

"Le rappeliste," he screamed, "ou est-ce?"

I motioned down, straight down.

"How many?" he asked. Moments later his partner gave a yell and cut their haul bag loose—an enormous black bag booming off slabs. It hit the talus with a sharp concussion and exploded, scattering gear for thirty feet. For the next few hours we could hear them yelling at each other in the darkness, trying to find the rappel anchors.

Aaron's watch alarm woke us well before dawn and we started climbing. Back up into Dolt Hole—this time no shit smeared about. Aaron took the long running swing and made it into the Stoveleg cracks on his second try and I led the off-width pitch he'd led for me the time before. I built a bombproof anchor in a three-inch-wide crack and got my butt comfortably into my belay seat. My hands were still intact and Aaron was working away down below. As I waited, it occured to me that on Half Dome I'd always felt as though if all the gear disappeared, I'd just be standing on some ledge. It'd be a lousy place to be standing, and I'd have plenty of time to disintegrate emotionally and psychologically, but someone would eventually come; I could probably even sit down while I waited.

Not so, the Nose. If the gear disappeared, I'd plummet. The wall above swooned. A day and a half up it, and three more to go—like being in the Pacific Ocean in a rowboat—no way to just go get an ice cream cone instead. My balance slipped and my knee scraped across the white granite; I leaned close and could see tiny bits of skin among the rugosities. All those swings on skinny little ropes all over again. Hanging on gear. My whole life. What if an old bolt popped or a knot in a sling worked its way loose? Such petty events with such ridiculous consequences.

I leaned out and looked up. The daily wind started to pick up; it cooled the sunburn on my neck and nose. Death thoughts started flooding in and I knew I was lost. It started in my stomach and spread—the stupidity of such risk in the name of recreation. What about books? Coffee? Sex? Friendships I wanted to maintain? Surfing and skiing were just weeks away and I wanted to live for them. I visualized floating off the lip of a head-high wave at Steamer Lane, telemarking in hip-deep champagne. So what if hundreds of climbers (maybe thousands?) had done this most tame, this most known of El Cap routes? This was insanity I had no capacity to tolerate. When I'd jugged up to Aaron he took one look at my face and knew what I was thinking.

"No worries," he said. I took a good look at him as I hung on the rope, covered with slings and carabiners, hooked-up, tied-in, locked-on to our elaborate web of safety. I stared at Aaron and breathed, rotated a bit as I dangled. It was too sudden, too easy an agreement. No anger, no reproach, not even a little disappointment. Maybe he was worn out himself and finally needed to stop pushing. He looked up at me with a light grin and sleepy eyes and said it was too late to rappel today, that we might as well head to Dolt Tower, bivy, and rap in the morning.

"You going to regret it?" I asked. I knew I would eventually.

"No chance, dude." He looked so relieved; his shoulders fell forward just a bit and his eyes closed. "Terra plata," he mumbled, nodding. "My rat's fed."

"Mine too. Stuffed." I started to laugh.

"No shit." Aaron giggled for a moment, then held his face in his taped-up bloodied hands. He looked over his shoulder at the ground far below, then closed his eyes again

and blew out as if he'd been punched in the stomach. Without looking up he said, "Pretty weird behavior for humans."

"Quite."

That night on top of Dolt Tower we had cozy little
sleeping nooks formed by years of effort—big rocks moved
around to form sheltering walls on a flat ledge. The illusion
of protection from the elements, isolation from the void. I
tried to enjoy just having this much to do with the great
white wall.

"Hey Aaron," I said, opening a can of peaches, "what
happened after you left Amanda? You just walk out?"

He blew a breath through his big lips and shook his
head, squinted off into the distance. "You know," he began,
"that's the craziest part."

"Oh yeah?" I felt wonderfully secure on that big rock,
knowing I'd be going down in the morning. I thought
maybe I needed all of this, each failure was a slightly higher
push, a deeper foray. I knew I'd be back, but not for a long
time.

"Yeah," Aaron said, "I walked all drunk and pukey into
the woods. Dirt sticking to my tears and everything. Think
how hungry I had to be. Really cold where it was getting
dangerous. And you know what? I was really, really
depressed."

"Don't blame you." Kyla'd probably be cuddling up
with that skinny bastard right about now. Two little dots of
light appeared across the valley on Middle Cathedral
Rock—someone having a bad night. Aaron said he'd wandered off at dawn without saying good-bye. Apparently he'd

gotten so run down and hungry he couldn't walk straight. And he was about fifteen miles from the highway.

"You know what happened?" he asked.

"Huh?"

"Saw a rabbit."

"Yeah?"

"Yeah. In a meadow. I looked at it and it looked at me and I knew and it knew that I was going to kill it. With my bare hands." He looked over at me like he'd just confessed a great crime. "I know," he said, "it's terrible. I threw a hunk of rock at it and totally missed. Then I threw another one. Missed again. Got it on the third try. When I picked it up it was all soft and warm. Even pretty cute. I felt awful."

"That keep you from eating it?"

"Nope." Far off along the Captain were little lights on the North America Wall. Probably two guys on a porta-ledge, guys who could live in space without fear.

"But I at least tried to thank the rabbit god. Just I didn't know his name. Man, I kept saying out loud how I was going to eat the whole thing and not waste anything. But I still felt horrible. I even thought how I eat burgers, so I should know what it means to kill. But still, no luck."

Aaron drank the last of the peach juice and reached for another can. We had a surplus of food; I even felt a little too full. I looked again at the North America Wall. It must've taken those guys years to be able put up with that much exposure. Aaron went on:

"So weird, Danny. I'm roasting the poor thing on this little spit over a fire, just minding my own business. Kind of nauseous but also starving. All of a sudden an entire tribe of coyotes starts howling in the woods. Oh, man, what a noise! Laughing and howling and barking and everything else and I just about lost my mind I got so scared. I was fully shaking." He leaned toward me and handed me the next can of peaches. "And you know what happened?" he asked.

"Tell me."

"I became mortal. Yep. I killed to eat, and the same could happen to me. When I realized that, I ate the whole bunny."

I took a long look at Aaron, then stood up on the ledge. My legs were cramped and my knees and hips burned with stiffness. I rubbed my eyes and looked up at this giant, disinterested beauty of a mountain. So many countless little unvisited corners and cracks, so many polished headwalls, smooth, soaring dihedrals. The headlamp over on the North America Wall blinked out. I wondered if they were falling asleep, or if perhaps they could see our lights over here. Maybe they could even see me standing with my arms spread out, wondering why I still wasn't ready for this thing and how I'd gotten it into my head that it mattered.

In the morning, rappelling back down those same airy bolt anchors, I heard a feminine voice say hello. I looked over from where I was hanging and saw the German woman's head poking out from behind the upper sickle of Sickle Ledge—a face in a rockscape.

"Why do you go down?" she asked.

"Oh," I said, "I got scared."

She smiled, then looked back into the corner where her partner apparently was. She looked back at me. "We are right now having big discussion," she said, and leaned back out of sight. A moment later, the German man's head appeared.

"Which is the way down?" he asked.

As we stumbled back from the rappels toward the car, we passed two lean, shirtless men marching purposefully toward the wall. We asked where they were headed.

"Sea of Dreams," one of them said, and marched on. I turned to watch them pass. Aaron never paused; he just walked on by. Near the start of the Nose, four young British men stood at the base with a huge pile of gear and water bottles. They looked at us with awe and curiosity—apparently we'd been up in that miraculous alternate universe, obviously we'd come down.

"What have you been on?" asked one with curly hair and little round glasses.

"The Nose," I said.

"Are you just finishing?"

"No," I said, "we came down."

"Why?" asked another, a fierce-looking boy with small blue eyes close together.

"I got scared," I said.

"Why?"

"Too big. Too steep."

The fierce one looked at me intensely, wondering who I was, whether this meant something about what lay in store for him, or simply something about me.

F i f t y

Naked, sunburnt, gaunt and smelly, Aaron and I splashed into the cold, snow-melt Merced River. We rubbed off dust and slipped butt-down, feet-first over little waterfalls, then dried off in the sun. Lying like lizards in the noon heat. Dry and clean, we drove out of Yosemite Valley. El Portal's few motels fed on the traffic, contributed nothing. Guests lay around swimming pools while twenty yards away the river—centerpiece of all they had come to see—poured over white granite slabs and formed wide, clear pools, all of them deserted.

On the north side of the canyon, opposite Route 140, the original road remained blasted into the rock. Parts of it had washed away, bridges over incoming gullies had collapsed. Rusting mining equipment stood out in the sun in front of an open shaft. That ancient metamorphic rock created grottoes and waterfalls in the river and kayakers stood by the water, laughing and waiting.

At Savage's Trading Post a roadsign indicated a place of historical interest:

Site of
SAVAGE'S TRADING POST

*Here in 1849 James D. Savage established a store built
of logs. He engaged in trading and mining and married several squaws for protection and influence. In Spring of 1850,
fearing Indian depredations, he moved to Mariposa creek. In
December his store and others were pillaged and burned and
a real war began. A volunteer battalion was formed and Savage was elected major. In pursuit of the most warlike tribe,
their secret hide-out, Yosemite Valley, was discovered and the
war brought to a quick end. Major Savage was killed by a
political opponent in 1852. Several years later his widow
guided John Hite, a poor prospector, a few miles up this south
fork to discover a gold mine that made him a millionaire.*

A store stood there with an inn. Inside were shelves of
Indian jewelry in jade and silver, death masks, war masks,
totem dolls, a taxidermed buffalo head, stylized spiritual art
for the New Age of white interest in shamanism, herbs, cof-
fees, rugs and without a trace of irony, Christmas tree balls
with Indian geometric patterns. The woman working the
store caught my eye, then spoke.

"You know," she said, raising her chin a bit, "I saw you
reading the sign outside. There's something you should
know. The Indians only fought back because miners started
strip-mining and dynamiting the river for fish. And the
squaws? Protection and influence? Give me a break."

And within a hundred years gasoline-soaked logs were

being thrown burning off Glacier Point to enhance the romantic quality of the valley.

As we leaned the Bug around the broad curves of the canyon, I had to cover my head with a wet T-shirt and keep nursing cold Cokes. Mariposa, like so many American towns, had preserved a two-block strip of nineteenth-century mainstreet with a western wooden sidewalk; and just beyond, the malls, parking lots and franchises insisted on names like Miner's Inn and Hitching Post. Billboards advertised Chinese Station Restaurant and somewhere called "Ol'Nip Gold Town," where you can go panning for nuggets. The road dropped fast from Mariposa, and soon we could see across the soft hills rolling down to the valley— gentle yellow curves with lone oaks. The hot afternoon air washed through the windows in arid, gentle waves.

At Cathy's Valley we passed the Chibchas Colombian restaurant; a stucco bungalo in quiet ranch country, it had a small garden outside with a fountain. Someone had planted a few willows to provide shade for more delicate plants. A concrete Bacchus stood among orange Indian paintbrush. Around the next turn in the highway, on a large gravel turnout with a view clear across the Central Valley to the Black Hills near Coalinga, Komfort had failed. The twenty-five-foot behemoth RV had overheated. Its adult crew was inside with shades drawn. A little barefoot boy walked gingerly around in the gravel turnout, looked up from time to time at the view.

Coming over the last ripples of the foothills, 140 straightened out, took on the survey-line feel of all Central

Valley roads. Rising and falling with the swells in the land, we approached a huge billboard. Out in the middle of all that dryness, by the side of the highway, the billboard screamed green. "Merced County," it said, "A Growing Place." Aaron pulled off into the gravel shoulder and slid to a stop. As the dust cleared, we stood and smelled the grass. Time, compressed by our speed, stretched out again. My feet hurt on the gravel. A McDonald's coffee cup lay on the ground.

The billboard also held out a welcome to Mariposa County. Planted amidst dry, blazing hot foothills, the sign depicted deep green hills like those of Ireland, a wide river meandering about and a rainbow splashing down in a pot of money. Beneath a gloved hand reaching into the pot were the words "Pure Gold." Behind those green hills loomed only one symbol of the vast Sierra High Country—an outline of Half Dome, the one piece of rock in that entire range that was still producing T-shirt dollars.

A dirt road meandered across the highway there at the county line. A dried-out barn with a corral lay unused in the waves of rustling grass; crickets cricked in the hot breeze. We walked across the hot asphalt and stood in front of a small wooden sign. All the paint had flaked off its incut letters; it said the old Millerton road had crossed here, the main nineteenth-century highway for goldseekers and settlers along the edge of the hills. The railroads changed the route, but the old road was still the county line.

A cattle truck rattled west at sixty-five miles an hour and blew my hair back. That hazy agricultural sky reddened the setting sun yet again. A motorcycle with a sidecar, black and chrome, roared east without a muffler. A bird picked up a current, hot air lifting in the evening, and drifted higher over the road. The highways struck me as straight and flawless, a flexible tarmac pulled out of a future warehouse and laid across ancient landscape. The waves of white history were so few, each so radically different from its precedent, that they butted against each other at a nowhere place on a nowhere road.

A few miles later the near-desert supported thousands of acres of walnut trees with no ground cover—naked dirt baking. Canals appeared: the aqueduct boondoggles. An L-shaped strip of eucalyptus in a fallow field sheltered the grave of a farmhouse from the northern winds. Past the railway the soaked, chemically enriched soil sustained tomatoes, strawberries, kiwis, peaches and apricots, lettuce to the horizon and no golden grass anywhere in sight. The ranch houses began to sprawl, their lawns widen. A man in front of a wide, low faux-brick home watered his RV. A Veterans Memorial obelisk stood outside a little town, its list of war dead longer than its Main Street. At the Apostolic Tabernacle a two-acre parking lot was full. The Shooting Range/Gunshop and Yosemite Wildlife Museum did brisk business—"You shoot 'em, we show 'em."

Before turning onto Interstate 5, before entering the big, straight L.A. to S.F. stream, we pulled off at the Kesterston Wildlife Reserve. The western atmosphere hung deep purple over the low black silhouette of the coastal mountains. Reserved were flat grasslands, bird habitat. A sign explained: "The U.S. Fish and Wildlife Service is responsible for protecting and preserving our country's wild birds, mammals and fish for the enjoyment of all people . . . to preserve our priceless wildlife heritage." Thus the permission of selenium at levels sufficient to wipe out nearly the entire local fishery. A whitewashed shack—closed down— sold hunting permits during the season. A pair of old jeans lay next to fresh vomit by the door.

Fifty-one

I'd just opened the apartment door and put down a milk crate when I heard a soft voice say, "Hi."

There on the futon, in the darkness, lay Kyla. She cleared her throat, and in the ambient light from the window I could see her sit up against the wall. The red light on my answering machine blinked three times.

"Naomi won't share," she said. I think she looked at my eyes after she spoke, but I couldn't see well enough to be sure. As I pushed the rest of my boxes in from the hallway, Kyla told me how they'd been loading seedlings into the bus when the Sykes Hot Springs trip came up. Naomi had flipped, and Chris hadn't even told her they'd slept together.

"But I'm really serious," Kyla insisted, "it's not really a sexual thing. I'm not even that attracted to him." I sat down on the floor and pulled off my disgusting, damp running shoes. I leaned against my bookcase and got a shelf up under my shoulder blades. Kyla had put all the chairs in storage. With the plants and dried flowers gone, the room just smelled of the garbage I'd forgotten to take out.

Naomi had stopped the loading and demanded a ceremony.

"I guess Christopher didn't really ask her like he said, or they misunderstood each other or something," Kyla said. I looked for tears on her cheeks in the faint light. I couldn't see any. Fog had dulled the glow from the streetlamps outside. "She laid all these guilt trips on me about how she never really had any friends before me and how mean her mom and dad were. It's like, whatever."

I pulled at the edge of the remaining climbing tape on my right hand. A few hairs stuck to it.

"Chris is kind of weird too," she continued. "He was all like 'Don't tell her we slept together,' you know, all about how it won't help anything and how she's pissed that he even asked permission."

I yanked hard and a whole strip of hair came off with the tape. I asked about that phone call to Oregon. Kyla wondered about that too.

She told me how Naomi got her ceremony: sage burned to rid the little house of evil spirits (leave a window open, so they can escape), pot smoked as a peace pipe, mainly, not so much to get high as to get into the right space. Christopher sat on a pillow while Naomi looked Kyla up and down. Apparently she kept staring at Kyla's mouth.

"We need to talk," Naomi had said, clearing her throat, "about what each of us expects out of this relationship. We have a future together. Honesty has gotten us pretty far. Kyla?"

Christopher's skin had broken out, Kyla said, and he

had a new rash under his nose. Apparently he wouldn't look at Kyla. He kept playing with a hollow wooden pear he'd carved for their daughter. I'd picked the thing up once too; a beautifully fashioned piece of fruit, testament to Chris's expert hands, it had a little hinged door on it and you could put different things inside.

"I told her how we wanted to include her," Kyla said, "and about all three of us being together. But I also told her me and Chris made love. I couldn't lie."

I gripped another strip of tape between my teeth and yanked. Little bits of adhesive were still glued into my wrinkles. A scab had come off to, and I licked the raw spot.

"Then Naomi started giving me all this shit again about her parents until like a minute later she realized what I'd said. I honestly watched her toe-knuckles turn all white and her whole face was like quivering."

I played a game with myself while Kyla talked, imagining I was Naomi, imagining I was in the room and that I saw that fading, cheap medieval serpent on Chris's arm and finally put one and two together.

"She's kind of ridiculous," Kyla said. "She really flipped. She's always been kind of unstable, even when we were kids, she'd have these temper tantrums. She like screamed at Chris how he was a compulsive liar, which he's not. He just has different visions of love. And she like screamed at me to get out of the house. She honestly even started throwing things. I feel so sorry for her baby, having to grow up in an environment like that."

I still had the Nose topo in my pocket. The advice scrawled all over it had smeared a little, but the map remained more or less intact. I took a pen off the bookcase and started to mark which pitches I'd led.

"It seemed like such an overreaction," Kyla said. She spread her legs apart and began to stretch. "I mean, those feelings between me and Chris were there. They weren't going to just go away. You can't just ignore stuff like that."

Naomi had ordered Kyla to leave and had called a council to decide about Oregon. Kyla knew exactly how the ceremony would go—they'd hold it in the group house in the room with the altar. Shari, now a successful color therapist in Monterey, would be there, and so would Gary, whose girlfriend had never come back from Hawaii. Naomi would pass a tray of incense sticks around the room and each person would light one as an offering to Air. On the carpet, Naomi would place a bowl of water with a stone in it for Water and Earth, and she'd light four tall candles on the altar for Fire. Chris would make a last attempt to patch things up, to bring Kyla along. He'd try to show that Kyla's love for him was love for Naomi too.

I asked what they'd decided.

"Press the button on the answering machine," she said.

After the first beep, my mom came on asking if I could meet for coffee. Then Nick let me know the first big northwest swell of the season was in, that the surf at Steamers was going off. When it beeped a third time, Kyla got up to get a glass of water, having heard it all before. As she walked past me her calves looked strong and she wore a thin green tank top that stopped just above her navel. The familiar smell of her body was still there.

And then Naomi came on, speaking into our almost empty studio from the little plastic machine on the floor. Her voice was shaking and imperious. "In crisis," she announced, "a community goes to the elders. But we don't have any, so I called a council of brothers and sisters." She coughed once, and an engine turned over in the background. "We want you to stay in California. You're not welcome on the farm."

F i f t y - t w o

Ocean, mist and sky are all gray with an early fall storm as I paddle out to a break north of Santa Cruz. Waves bigger than I've ever surfed explode off the cliff and surge across shelves of shale and into caves. As the rows of long, swelling walls lift up into still air they catch diffuse sunlight and glow as organic undulations of molten silver.

The tide is dropping so quickly that big outside sets keep breaking farther and farther out to sea. I have to paddle for about an hour straight to stay out of the impact zone. The effort keeps me warm in the frigid water and I can taste the salt. Finally, I surge up over the lip of a face three times my height and am safe. Out beyond the peak I can rise and fall unafraid. Two sea otters wrestle no more than fifteen feet from my board, batting each other's ears and rolling one another under water. Seven pelicans glide in single file along the cushion of air pushed before a wave, then soar away from the breaking foam. Just as the whole wall next to them crashes they lift as a body into the air.

Kyla called this morning to say hello. She's living with a pot grower in Compche, helping him trim bud for the fall harvest. She says she needs the work; she's trying not to tap into her trust fund too much. She doesn't think it'll last with him, so she's thinking about coming down to Berkeley for a while.

I can see a big wave growing up off the outer reef—a warping, shining line. Dusk sunlight spreads through an opening in the clouds and spatters the colors of a New England autumn across the water. I paddle toward the wave until I'm certain it won't break on top of me, then turn around and start stroking with it. It lifts my board slowly at first, then suddenly sweeps me up and away from the water below. In the moment before I'd crash forward in the curl, I step to my feet on the board and lean down into the slope.

Like jumping off an avalanching cornice on skis, I fall to the right. At the wave's base, the mass of its energy lifting overhead, I channel the board's speed along the wall. As I fly forward, barely keeping my balance as the board skips like a stone, the wave far ahead begins to steepen into an enormous bowl. It's going to crash ahead of me as well as behind, and I'll be thrown forward and held under. I cut high, rip along in the spray, shoot down to the base to pick up speed, and then, just as the lip begins to throw over forward, I carve up the face. My body comes over the top as the lip grabs the board from my feet. Momentum carries me high over the trough behind the wave.

COLOPHON

This book was designed by Foos Rowntree. The text is set in
Fairfield type, a roman originally designed in the early 1940s by
Rudolf Ruzicka. The chapter headings and parts of
the front cover and title page are set in Temperance Mono.
The composition is by The Typeworks. The book
was manufactured by Maple-Vail on acid-free paper.